"With her creative vignettes about the Pewsitters, Katherine Hussmann Klemp shares warm, personal, and faith-filled meditations. Each anticipatory vignette introduces a glimpse of God's mysterious work in the everyday lives of His people. These creative vignettes offer practical and useful 'hooks' for those who plan Bible studies and devotional thoughts in a variety of church settings. What a wonderful new tool for those who teach and learn!"

Mary Cash Hilgendorf, PhD
Director, Women's Leadership Institute Professor of Education,
Concordia University Wisconsin

"These skits and devotions are a wonderful blessing from God. Your faith will be strengthened and your library of humor will be enlarged. A job well done."

Tom Braun, Pastor,
Christ Victorious Lutheran Church, Chaska, MN

"Katherine Klemp's *Pewsitters* is an innovative and fresh approach to the daily devotion. Presenting both skit and devotion together brings a tangible aspect that allows for a deeper understanding of her daily scriptural lessons. I was moved to take a good look at my own walk with the Lord and was genuinely inspired!"

Theresa Schneider, Editor in Chief, EZRA Publications

"Ever watch on TV—probably inadvertently—a sensationalistic reporting of some rank outbreak of sin and degradation? And then you felt like you needed to take a shower?

Read one of these tandem combos of skits-and-devotions by Katherine Klemp. It'll be a refreshing, cleansing experience for your soul. Ingest and enjoy. Use them in worship services (especially the skits), small group meetings, or just for your personal edification."

Dr. Deane Schuessler, author, *Devoted to God and Each Other*

The
PEWSITTERS

The
PEWSITTERS

Skits & Devotions for Church & Home

Katherine Hussmann Klemp

Tate Publishing & Enterprises

The Pewsitters
Copyright © 2008 by Katherine Hussmann Klemp. All rights reserved.

This title is also available as a Tate Out Loud product. Visit www.tatepublishing.com for more information.

Unless otherwise noted, Scripture quotations are taken from the *Holy Bible, New International Version* ®, Copyright © 1973, 1978, 1984 by International Bible Society. Used by permission of Zondervan Publishing House. All rights reserved.

Scripture quotations marked "NLT" are taken from the *Holy Bible, New Living Translation,* Copyright © 1996. Used by permission of Tyndale House Publishers, Inc. All rights reserved.

Scripture quotations marked "NKJV" are taken from *The New King James Version/* Thomas Nelson Publishers, Nashville: Thomas Nelson Publishers. Copyright © 1982. Used by permission. All rights reserved.

The opinions expressed by the author are not necessarily those of Tate Publishing, LLC.

This book contains descriptions of situations and events that are recounted as accurately as possible from the author's memory. The names of those involved have been changed in order to protect their privacy.

Published by Tate Publishing & Enterprises, LLC
127 E. Trade Center Terrace | Mustang, Oklahoma 73064 USA
1.888.361.9473 | www.tatepublishing.com
Tate Publishing is committed to excellence in the publishing industry. The company reflects the philosophy established by the founders, based on Psalm 68:11,
"The Lord gave the word and great was the company of those who published it."
Book design copyright © 2008 by Tate Publishing, LLC. All rights reserved.
Cover design by Lindsay B. Behrens
Interior design by Stephanie Woloszyn

Published in the United States of America
ISBN: 978-1-60462-543-1
1. Church & Ministry:Church Life:Prog.
2. Ministry Resources: Teaching Help

08.01.18

Dedication

To Christian parents.

The Reverend Otto B. Hussmann and Bertha (nee Steffen) Hussmann who brought me to know my Savior, Jesus, at a very early age,

and to my husband, Paul, who has always encouraged me to pursue my dreams.

Lord, I long to be a branch
Grafted to Your mighty vine,
Unconcerned with fruit or leaves,
Happy there to just be Thine.

Gracious Lord, I find my rest
Nourished through your fruitful stem.
May I be a faithful guest,
My daily food, the Great Amen.

Let Your fruit that bends my branch
Overflow to great and least,
That those who eat this yield, there find,
A foretaste of Your Heavenly Feast.

John 15:5

Katherine Hussmann Klemp
April 30, 2007

Table of Contents

Preface

I once read that if you hear the same comment from fellow Christians more than twice, it would be well to pay attention to what they are saying. After all, God speaks to us through other Christians. Well, for the past twenty years or so, people have been telling me, "You should write a book."

At first I did not take these remarks seriously. Later on I began to wonder. I would ask my friends, "Do you have a lot of people telling you to write a book?"

Most would look at me blankly and then say, "No one has ever told me to write a book."

I found that hard to believe. Surely people were not speaking specifically to me. Surely this was something people just said to other people who told a funny story or related a crazy situation they had just experienced.

But then I started writing. A couple joined our church and brought with them the clever idea of a group of people who would talk among themselves before the church service begins—just regular folks who sit in the same pew Sunday after Sunday. And so we began to have little skits with these "pew sitter" folks.

The couple, Dan and Elizabeth Decker, moved on less than a year later, but The Pewsitters stayed behind. I was given the assignment to write the skits, and, for nearly a decade, I have been doing just that. My husband, Paul, and I were the original Leon and Estelle and stayed in those roles until we moved to the St. Paul, Minnesota, area a couple of years ago. I still write the scripts for the Pewsitters, but now a new Leon and a new Estelle are at our old church, Christ Victorious Lutheran Church in Chaska, Minnesota. Thanks to the wonderful technology of e-mail we haven't missed a beat.

Then, about a year ago, I was asked to be a devotion writer for a Christian Web site, ezraweb.com. I found this to be an exciting opportunity to serve God through writing. In the way that only God can lead, these two ministries dovetailed beautifully, and *The Pewsitters* is the result.

So, I finally listened, and I wrote a book. God does move in a mysterious way, His wonders to perform. This book is proof of that!

Katherine Hussmann Klemp
June 25, 2007

Pewsitter Savvy

These skits and devotions are meant to deepen your relationship with your Lord Jesus. The more we know about one another, the more we appreciate one another. And, in order to know Jesus better, we must look carefully at His Word. Some of us have formed ideas about God that are not at all what He has revealed to us. Sometimes those assumptions lead us to doubt God and His love for us. The devotions are based on scripture and are designed to lead to a fuller understanding of the true God and Jesus Christ, whom the Father has sent.

In addition, as you use these devotions, either alone or with other Christians, you will be led into a position of reverence for your Lord and Savior. The more we know Him, the more we love Him. The more we know of Him, the more we stand in awe of the mighty things He has done on our behalf. Hannah Whitehall Smith wrote a book entitled, *The Christian's Secret to a Happy Life*. *The Pewsitters* is intended to shed some light on this "secret" as well, for Proverbs 28 says, "Happy is the man who is always reverent" (Proverbs 28:14, NKJV).

There is no wrong way or right way to use the material. I have used the skits as an opening to a meeting by simply assigning four of the people present to read right from where they were sitting, and I have pulled people out of the group to sit in front in a row of chairs to simulate a pew. I have seen the characters use costumes and have seen them come just as they are. At our church, the same four people play the characters each Sunday before the sermon so that it has become an ongoing saga. Sometimes a little boy sits with the group, and occasionally one of the regulars is not in church, as is the case in real life. Thus, there are several minor characters that you will also get to know. A rehearsal for us means everyone prints off the script that was e-mailed to them so that they are familiar with their part before coming to church and then we read it aloud once or twice in the lobby. No more preparation than that is needed.

Have fun with the scripts. As you read through the skits, you will see that they are fairly generic. I usually use two men and two women, but often it could be a conversation between four men or four women. Occasionally, there is a child in the script. When you choose people for the parts, you can have a man play a woman or a woman play a man, an adult a child, and your youth can act like adults. In your family devotions, family members may be assigned a character to play each time, or the roles may be passed around. You can use props and costumes to enhance the characters (sometimes a simple hat will do), or you can pull four people out of a meeting to read the script on the spot. If I mention Minnesota, you can rename it Montana or California if it makes it more personal to your audience that way. You can use the devotions or prayers I have included or write your own. You can use the devotion and not the skit. The bottom line is that you can do what makes most sense in your situation.

The characters are normal people having the normal conversations that people would have. So basically, if you want to cast it right, find some normal people (easier said than done, I know) who are not afraid to be in front of a group, who can speak loudly enough so that everyone can hear, and go from there. Or just use whoever is at hand. Personally, I like the scripts read rather than memorized. There is a certain consistency when all are reading that allows the message to come across clearly. Once again, do as you like.

To God be the glory.

Synopsis

We find here a group of people who attend the same church and are in the habit of sitting together in the same pew each week. The "pewsitters" talk to one another about things that concern them or things that caught their attention in the previous week. They know each other pretty well.

Characters

LEON. A mature gentleman. Mature in age as well as in understanding of Scripture. Leon is always kind, always Christian. He is comfortable with himself and is concerned for others, sometimes funny, but never flip. He is a wonderful example of a lifetime follower of Christ.

ESTELLE. A mature Christian in age and understanding of the Bible's teachings. Estelle can be judgmental at times, but knows better. She hates change and is sometimes kind to the younger "pewsitters" and sometimes impatient with their exuberance and youth.

VAUGHN. A strong, but struggling Christian young man in his twenties. Vaughn went to church with his parents as a child, but did not come to know Christ as his personal Savior until after an aimless youth. He now wants to be a strong man of God, but is living in an age that seldom applauds his desire to know and serve God. He is growing in leaps and bounds, yet sometimes he doesn't "get it," even though you think he should.

JULIE. In the middle of raising her family. Church is important to her, but life takes quite a toll, pulling her in a million different directions. She is a delightful and thoughtful young woman. Julie is well-versed in her faith, but she, like Vaughn, has many non-Christian coworkers and friends.

DIXIE. A young woman who knows little about church. She came because the pastor invited her. Probably in a poor marriage, she has several small children. Dixie has a transparent nature, i.e., what you see is what you get. She is a little "ditzy," but not unkind. Dixie is searching for more meaning in her life. She likes to sit with the Pewsitters when she comes to church (which is not often).

DANNY. A ten-year-old boy who is serious about learning more about God. He is slightly mischievous and full of energy.

ALAN and LISA. A couple, married for some time. They are strong in their faith and are both trying to live Christian lives.

Props

Four or five chairs set up to resemble a pew. Or, better yet, a pew, if it's available.

Costumes

None needed, but you may use various styles of clothing to suggest your character.

Sound

Microphones, if you wish. None are necessary in a smaller setting.

Lighting

As you wish.

Setting

Sunday morning in a familiar pew in church, or friends sitting and talking together at a church gathering of some kind.

Director's Tip

I have the characters read the script during the skit. That way, the attention is on the message. If you want to memorize and be more dramatic, you may.

God Mysteriously at Work

VAUGHN. I had an interesting day yesterday. I won a lawn mower.

ESTELLE. Wow, that's great! I usually don't enter contests because I don't think anybody wins those things anyway. Maybe I should start.

JULIE. What kind of contest was it?

VAUGHN. It wasn't really a contest. The new hardware store just down from me was having a grand opening. As I was going in I held the door for an elderly lady to go ahead of me, and when I went in the bells went off and balloons went up and people started clapping. I was the one thousandth customer for their new store.

LEON. I'll bet the lady you so kindly let in wasn't too happy with that.

VAUGHN. Well, she did give me a few whacks with her purse. I only went in because I was driving by and remembered I needed a couple of AA batteries.

LEON. Thin threads. Sort of a variation on the stories of people who just barely miss their flights at an airport and then find out that the plane they missed crashed on takeoff.

JULIE. I can tell you a good story like that. My sister lost her husband about seven years ago. Last January she finally decided to go to Hawaii on her own. It was a trip she and her husband had always talked about taking together. While she was gone, her house burned down.

ESTELLE. That's terrible. Is *that* the unexpected thing? I mean, if she hadn't gone to Hawaii her house would still be here?

JULIE. No, not that. The thin thread is that the insurance adjustor who came to appraise the house was her old boy-friend from high school. He had never married, and now they are seriously dating.

VAUGHN. She might never have met up with him again without that fire happening.

LEON. That's quite a story, Julie. You know, God has His hand on every aspect of our lives. Whatever happens is a part of His plan for us.

ESTELLE. And if it's in His plan, whatever it is, it's for our good.

God Mysteriously at Work

Jesus replied, "You do not realize now what I am doing, but later you will understand."

John 13:7

How often have you wrestled with God over an issue that is very important to you—a health problem, the loss of a loved one, a troubled marriage, an addiction, an important financial decision, a son or daughter who has wandered from their faith? I cannot count the number of times I have promised God that I am content to leave things in His loving hands; that I am willing to rest in His choices for my life. Why, then, do I snatch the problem right back and start to worry about it again?

Part of it is a lack of faith. But much of it has to do with the fact that God's ways of doing things are not my ways of doing things. In John 13:6, Peter asks Jesus, "Lord, are you going to wash my feet?"

Jesus explains, "You do not realize now what I am doing, but later you will understand" (John 13:7).

And what is Peter's response? "No," says Peter, "you shall never wash my feet" (John 13:8).

At first glance, Peter's response seems to be one of humility. He did not want His Lord and Master to provide such a lowly act of service for someone as insignificant and sinful as he. On further examination, however, we realize that it was really an act of pride. Peter found it humbling for Jesus to wash his feet and was too proud to allow it, even after Jesus had given him an explanation. "You do not realize now what I am doing" (John 13:7a).

Aren't we just like that? In essence, God says, "Trust Me. Understand that you may not understand, but I see the whole picture, you do not. Someday you will, but for right now, just believe that I have a plan that is meant for your good."

And we, like Peter, say, no. That was not a good enough answer for Peter, and it is often not good enough for us either.

"Why would a good God allow this to happen?" we lament.

"You do not realize now what I am doing" is Jesus' loving reply.

"If God is in charge here, why have so many evil people become rich and powerful and so many believers become poor and persecuted?" we ask in indignation.

"You do not realize now what I am doing," He answers patiently.

We want more of an explanation. We don't like to give up control of our lives, and perhaps for good reason. C. S. Lewis says, "We're not necessarily doubting that God will do the best for us; we are wondering how painful the best will turn out to be." After all, God's ways are not our ways.

As difficult as it is for Peter to swallow his pride, he does so quickly when He hears Jesus' next words: "Unless I wash you, you have no part with me" (John 13:8).

God's ways are mysterious. His thoughts are higher than our thoughts. And we, like Peter, need to swallow our pride, our faulty sense of being right, and our love of control and submit to Him. He has revealed His great love for us by sending His only Son as our Redeemer. Jesus' sacrifice put us back into a right relationship with the Father. And our Heavenly Father has a perfect plan for each of us. That is all we need to know in order to trust Him with our health, our finances, our joys, and our sorrows.

And, having placed ourselves in His care, we cling to Jesus' promise, "later you will understand" (John 13:7).

Heavenly Father, forgive us for doubting Your love. We often struggle with the way things happen here on earth. We are afraid to "let go and let God," as many have urged us to do, because we like things to go "our way." Remind us often that Your ways are mysterious to us, that they are higher than our ways, that You see the big picture, and that we will not know the full outcome of the events of our lives until we get to heaven. Help us to be obedient children, fully aware that Your plans for our lives are good plans. We rest in the promise of Your love through Christ Jesus our Lord. Amen.

In Season and Out of Season

VAUGHN. I don't know if I told you this, but my wife and I have been doing family devotions pretty regularly for the past few months.

LEON. That's great, Vaughn. That's a very good way to become strong in your faith.

JULIE. I wish we had more time. We get pretty spotty with them.

ESTELLE. My husband and I decided that family devotions were going to be an important part of our lives. We've been able to stay at it pretty consistently all these years.

VAUGHN. I have to admit that I thought it was a good idea, but I didn't expect it to change me.

LEON. God's Word is powerful.

VAUGHN. No kidding. Yesterday a buddy of mine was complaining and complaining about all sorts of stuff. Finally, I said, "This is the day the Lord has made; let us rejoice and be glad in it."

ESTELLE. A good answer, Vaughn.

VAUGHN. Yeah, well, he looked at me for a moment, and then asked, "Do you really believe that stuff?" And I witnessed my faith to him.

JULIE. Good for you, Vaughn.

VAUGHN. It kind of freaked me out. I mean, where did that come from? I'm not one that speaks out for Jesus very often, so I was just as surprised as my friend was.

LEON. It's as though God took you, a normally tongue-tied Christian, and put right into your mouth the words you needed to share your faith.

VAUGHN. My buddy didn't laugh or mock me or anything. He said he could see that I had something that made my life seem richer than his, and he even asked a few questions. I'm looking forward to some good conversations about Jesus with him in the future.

JULIE. From now on we are going to find time for devotions at our house. I want to be full of God's Word, ready to speak about Jesus to my friends too.

In Season and Out of Season

Brethren, if anyone among you wanders from the truth, and someone turns him back, let him know that he who turns a sinner from the error of his way will save a soul from death and cover a multitude of sins.

James 5:19–20 (NKJV)

I remember, years ago, talking with the wife of one of my husband's friends. This woman's husband and mine were off doing some project or another out in the garage, and the two of us were visiting over a cup of coffee in the kitchen. This was the first time we had met, so the conversation was going wherever it took us, and, for some reason, it took us to the topic of abortion.

I made the statement that I thought abortion was wrong, and she argued for the other side. The discussion was not heated; rather, it became a thoughtful debate, she giving the arguments she had heard concerning a woman's right to choose, and I witnessing to the Bible's teachings. We parted amicably. We saw this couple only once again in our marriage. Our husbands had finished their mutual project, and we moved back out of one another's lives.

Some years later I received a letter from this woman. In it, she told of how she had become pregnant, and since she was in her late thirties, the doctor wanted to do an amnio-centesis (a test for birth defects before a baby is born). The test results showed that the child had Down's syndrome, a form of mental retardation. The doctor counseled that the wisest course for this couple would be to abort the child.

In her letter, she noted that she had remembered our con-versation, and, after research of her own, had decided to keep the child. She was writing, she said, to thank me. She described the peace she experienced knowing that she had made a God-pleasing decision and went on to tell of the joy this child had already brought to their home in the past four years.

Now, let's reread the passage above: "Brethren, if anyone among you wanders from the truth, and someone turns him back, let him know that he who turns a sinner from the error of his way will save a soul from death and cover a multitude of sins" (James 5:19–20, NKJV).

Does that give you goose bumps, or what? Yet how many times do we subscribe to the world and Satan telling us that speaking the truth is being judgmental? Have we ever let a Christian friend pursue a path that we know is harmful, but we don't want to bring up something that might hurt our friendship? How many conversations have we limited to non-controversial subjects in order to keep the peace? Is this good manners or a lack of love for others?

Or perhaps a love of self? We get self-protective. We don't want to suffer the anger or bad opinion of others. But, if God is to be believed, the opposite occurs. People do turn from sin. They often find the deep Christian concern of others not only welcome, but an essential ingredient for living a faithful life.

Second Timothy 4:2 reads, "Preach the Word; be prepared in season and out of season; correct, rebuke, and encourage—with great patience and careful instruction."

So, from now on, let us resolve to let God be the conversation leader when we speak with others. He knows what people need to hear. We need to be willing to speak of the things of God, both in season and out of season, with great patience and careful instruction. God can and does change people's hearts through our faithful obedience. And this may lead wandering folks to turn from the error of their ways and save their souls from death, thus covering a multitude of sins.

Heavenly Father, we want to be faithful. From now on make our conversations with others rich with thoughts and words from You. You have promised that Your Word does not return to You void. Keep us ever mindful of the cry for help emanating from those around us. And thank You, Lord, for the privilege of being Your messengers to the world. In Jesus' name we pray. Amen.

"Right" from the Start

LEON. Well, Danny, what did you think of the Old Testament lesson today? God had a big task for a very young Jeremiah, didn't he?

DANNY. All I can say is, "I am only a youth."

JULIE. Yeah, Jeremiah tried that approach, too, but God did not accept that excuse or give him something simpler to do. Instead, he was asked to be a prophet to the nations, and that was that. God was calling.

DANNY. I hope God doesn't have some big plan for me.

LEON. He has big plans for each of us.

ALAN. I know how both Danny and Jeremiah felt. I don't think I have ever told anyone this story, but, when I was ten years old, a friend of mine invited me to come to Sunday school with him. My mom and dad were not church people in any way. My dad just laughed when I asked if I could go along that first time. He said it was okay, but I could tell he didn't think much of church.

JULIE. You've gone to church ever since I've known you. Is that when you became a Christian?

ALAN. Yes, it is. I fell in love with God within a Sunday or two. I loved having a Savior who loved me. I felt happy and safe, and then it happened.

DANNY. What happened?

ALAN. Then God laid it on my heart that I was to bring the message of His love and forgiveness to my family.

DANNY. When you were ten?

ALAN. I used that excuse over and over. I kept telling God, "I'm too young. They'll never listen to me." But God kept telling me that I was the one. I was never so scared in my life.

JULIE. But ever since I've known you, your whole family has gone to this church. I think your dad was an elder when we first met.

DANNY. You mean they listened to you, Alan?

ALAN. Well, I know they listened to God's calling. He had promised if I would trust Him, He would do the rest.

JULIE. God has big plans for us whether we are young or not so young. If we are willing, He is able.

DANNY. Well, if I'm going to be God's messenger to the world, I guess I'd better start right now.

LEON. A good start, if you ask me!

"Right" from the Start

Remember your Creator in the days of your youth, before the days of trouble come and the years approach when you will say, "I find no pleasure in them."

Ecclesiastes 12:1

For some kids, King Solomon's words seem uninformed when he says, "in the days of your youth, before the days of trouble come."

"Follow me around for one day," they would like to tell him. "I'll show you trouble."

And yet, according to the Bible, Solomon was the wisest man who ever lived. So there must be something here that we are missing. For one thing, Solomon, not only the wisest, but the richest man that ever lived, had seen it all, achieved it all, had it all. He denied himself nothing that would bring him pleasure. He did many great things in his life. Architecture and biology were two of many areas where he excelled. But he also did sinful things, such as worshiping false idols and having many wives and concubines.

Actually, though, he had done what he is advising us to do. He had remembered his Creator in the days of his youth. As King David's son, he was the one who built the temple that his father had always wanted to build. He was the one

God told to ask whatever he wanted and it would be his. And he pleased God when he asked for wisdom to rule the people.

Have you ever heard of the butterfly effect? Wikipedia. com defines it this way: "The phrase refers to the idea that a butterfly's wings might create tiny changes in the atmosphere that ultimately cause a tornado to appear (or, for that matter, prevent a tornado from appearing). The flapping wing represents a small change in the initial condition of the system, which causes a chain of events leading to large-scale phenomena. Had the butterfly not flapped its wings, the trajectory of the system might have been vastly different."

The idea is that the way we do things now produces a much larger effect as time goes by. Not long ago I read that if you start a project and get the first 10–15% of the project right, it will probably turn out okay, even if there are things that go wrong later.

I think that happened for King Solomon. He got the first part of his life right with God, but he often strayed in his middle and later years. Thus, when he reviewed his life in the book of Ecclesiastes, he wrote: "'Meaningless. Meaningless!' says the Teacher. 'Everything is meaningless!'"(Ecclesiastes 12: 8).

Nevertheless, because he got the first part of his life right, he was able to hold on to his belief in God through all the doubts and detours and troubles. His final conclusion, only five verses later, reads: "Fear God and keep his commandments, for this is the whole duty of man" (Ecclesiastes 12:13).

I hope you see the importance of keeping God in the center of your life now, while you are young. "Remember your Creator in the days of your youth, before the days of trouble come," in the sure hope that you will be able to be faithful right up to the day you die and receive from Jesus the crown of life.

Dear Lord, we come asking that You keep us firm in our faith, especially now, while we are young. We want to love and serve You all the days of our lives. Help us to follow You from our early years until our final hours, that You may be praised for sending Jesus as our Redeemer and Friend. Make us a blessing to many by getting it right, right from the start. In Jesus' name we pray. Amen.

Peace at Last

VAUGHN. What do you think heaven is going to be like?

LEON. For one thing, most of the glimpses of heaven the Bible gives us include worship.

ESTELLE. I know the Bible talks about cherubim and seraphim around the throne singing words of praise.

JULIE. When I think of heaven, I think of peace. I could use a little peace about now.

VAUGHN. What's not peaceful in your life right now, Julie? Are you worried about the war in Iraq?

JULIE. No, I'm worried about the war in (insert name of town in which you live)—the one with my neighbors next door.

LEON. It must be serious if you refer to it as a war.

JULIE. Well, they've done some downright unforgivable things. I'm not going into specifics, but this whole thing has been eating at me for a couple of weeks already.

ESTELLE. I think I know a way to make the peace.

JULIE. Fat chance! You don't know these people. They're not going to change no matter how reasonable you get.

ESTELLE. I wasn't thinking of changing *them*.

LEON. I'll bet I know what you're getting at, Estelle. You can't change their attitude, Julie, but with Jesus' help, you can change your own.

VAUGHN. Let it go. Forgive them.

JULIE. Easier said than done.

LEON. It's never easy, but, when we ask for God's power to forgive as we've been forgiven, we don't have to wait to go to heaven to get some peace.

JULIE. I've been so busy going over and over how right I am and how wrong they are that, not only have I not thought of forgiving them, I haven't asked God to forgive me for my bitterness. Thanks for the reminder, everyone. I'd forgotten how healing forgiveness can be.

ESTELLE. I have found that once I forgive and am forgiven, I am not only at peace, but I am once again ready and able to serve my Lord with joy.

Peace at Last

A man's wisdom gives him patience; it is to his glory
to overlook an offence.

Proverbs 19:11

As a young wife I remember how easily I could call to mind
all my husband's shortcomings. With each new offence,
I lengthened the list. Every time my feelings were hurt I
recounted a litany of grievances. I rehearsed that list often,
and I knew it by heart.

I do not do that so much anymore, and I see that as a sign
of God's love working in my heart. In fact, when I find myself
starting that old score-keeping process, I stop and ask myself
if I have drifted from God's side.

The writer of Proverbs says, "A man's wisdom gives him
patience; it is to his glory to overlook an offence." It is a good
feeling to let go of things others do that irritate you. It is even
more freeing to let go of a real hurt.

Some years ago my husband was ill. Several people whom
we counted on to be supportive became very concerned with
their own affairs and created a hardship for us. I find it interesting that I was able to let it go and have not thought of that
in a couple of years. And I find joy and gratitude in my heart
this day that something that happened so long ago has not

poisoned my life with grievance. It could have, and many of you know exactly what I am talking about.

What is that particular hurt (or list of hurts, for that matter) that is dominating your thinking right now? Have you been rolling the bad taste of it around in your mouth? Have you been poking at it with your tongue daily (or hourly) to taste the hurt once again, to feel the injustice of it all, to savor the rightness of your position and the wrongness of the other person's actions toward you?

Well, you may be enjoying your indignation, but the writer of Proverbs tells us there is glory in overlooking an offence. I'm not suggesting we can achieve this on our own. In the first chapter of Proverbs, we are told that the fear of the Lord is the beginning of wisdom. Our ability to overlook an offence is possible only when we seek God's power to forgive others. But the outcome is well worth giving up our self-pity. When forgiveness is at work within us, we not only experience the peace that passes understanding, but we know for sure that Christ's love is dwelling in us.

A man's wisdom comes from God. This true wisdom brings patience and the ability to overlook an offence. It is another of God's wonderful gifts to His children. This is the day the Lord has made. Let us rejoice and be glad in it, not sit in misery nursing our grievance toward others who have caused us harm. And, because of the power of God's forgiveness working in our hearts, we can do just that.

Peace at last.

Heavenly Father, forgive us for our unforgiving hearts. We often hold others to a standard of behavior to which we do not hold ourselves. We nurture grudges. We keep ledgers to tally the wrongs others commit against us. In times of real hurt, we do not even want to forgive. Your Son taught us to pray, "Forgive us our debts, as we forgive our debtors." We thank You that we can draw on Your power to forgive others, that we may live a peaceable life through Jesus Christ, our Lord. Amen.

Christ-Esteem

ESTELLE. Hi, everybody. How's it going?

JULIE. Not too good for me.

LEON. What's wrong, Julie?

JULIE. Nothing's wrong, exactly. It's just that I'm so frustrated at work. No matter what I do, Nichole, this girl in my office, gets her stuff in earlier, has a higher quota for the week, and month after month is held up as an example for the rest of us.

VAUGHN. I know what you mean. There was this guy, Karl, on my softball team this summer that could do it all. Not only was he our best pitcher, I can't tell you how many homeruns he hit. I felt like a real klutz around him.

ESTELLE. Well, why is that a problem?

JULIE. Why is that a problem? It's obvious that I have a problem.

ESTELLE. It's only a problem if you make it one.

VAUGHN. I don't see what you're getting at. I just don't measure up next to this guy. What part of that don't you understand, Estelle?

LEON. I think Estelle is asking both of you to think about what you just said and suggesting you might want to examine your feelings about not being the best. That's what this is about, isn't it? Being the best?

VAUGHN. Well, yeah.

JULIE. Are you telling us not to strive for excellence, Estelle?

ESTELLE. I'm just suggesting that maybe Jesus doesn't require us to be better than others.

LEON. Estelle's right, you know. Jesus rebuked his disciples for fighting over who was going to be greatest in the Kingdom of Heaven. The world tells us to put ourselves forward, but Jesus says the first shall be last and the last shall be first.

JULIE. You know, if I would rejoice in Nichole's skill and just be glad she's part of the team, I could really enjoy working with her instead of being resentful.

VAUGHN. Yeah, what am I complaining about? Karl's skills were a big reason we made it to the playoffs.

LEON. We don't have to be the best. Because Jesus bought us back from sin and death, we already have all the worth we will ever need.

Christ-Esteem

For it is not the one who commends himself who is approved, but the one whom the LORD commends.

2 Corinthians 10:18

I love sports. It is the contest itself that gets me hooked. One thing I have come to dread, though, is the self-congratulations of many contestants: the basketball player who points broadly at himself after making a difficult shot, the football player standing in the end zone, arms spread wide, urging the crowd to applaud more loudly, or the post-game interview where the golfer tells us what a great round he played.

We have all heard the hype about our children needing to gain self-esteem. The prevailing thought is to praise them often for work well (or even not so well) done. Then be sure to teach them to be their own cheerleaders. And, of course, avoid making them feel bad when they fail or do something wrong.

Unfortunately, none of this works because these tactics merely reinforce the child's sinful nature that screams, "Me. Me. *Me!*" So what we have done is raise self-centered children who are fully convinced the world should revolve around them. And most of these selfish children have poor self-esteem. After all, they know they are self-centered and self-serving, and they know it is nothing to be proud of.

Contrast that thinking with the passage St. Paul wrote to the Corinthians:"For it is not the one who commends himself who is approved, but the one whom the Lord commends."

I read a book some years ago called *Christ-Esteem*. The author, Donald Matzat, wrote that, until we experience the love and forgiveness of Christ Jesus, we all have a sense of unworthiness. Some people try to cover these feelings by being proud and arrogant, while others live lives of guilt and shame.

It is because Jesus came to die for us that we have the first glimpse of our worth. In Christ we become wanted and redeemed and holy and pure and loved. It is in Christ that we find our value.

Self-sacrifice, humility, servanthood—these are the bywords of "Christ-esteem." Living lives that reflect Christ's love brings joy. It allows us to get off the throne of our own hearts and let Christ live there instead.

We cannot earn our way into God's good graces, nor our own. So we need to quit trying to make our children (or ourselves) "think more highly of yourselves than you ought" (Romans 12:3). Instead, we must admit our unworthiness and ask God to rule in our hearts.

Self-esteem? No. Christ-esteem? Yes. For in Christ we have great worth. Through His redemption we have become beloved children of a King, fellow inheritors of the kingdom of God.

Heavenly Father, we come to You humbled to admit how much we shy away from feelings of shame. We often shield our children from the consequences of their behavior, mistakenly thinking we are building them up. We acknowledge this day that we have no worth apart from You, and yet we rejoice that we find value in Your eyes. While we were still sinners, You loved us enough to send Your Son to die for us. You redeemed us, not with gold or silver, but with something far more precious than that—the blood of Jesus Christ. Release us from our constant striving to feel good about ourselves and let us rest in You, knowing that in Christ we are loved and forgiven. We pray in the name of Jesus. Amen.

Inner Strength?

JULIE. I have a real challenging week ahead. Pray for me.

LEON. Sure, Julie. Is there anything we can do to help?

JULIE. No, I'm pretty sure I can handle it. I just have to dig deep within to pull out my best effort, and I think I'll be okay.

ESTELLE. I don't think that is a good idea, Julie.

VAUGHN. Are you kidding, Estelle? How can that not be a good idea? Don't you think she should pull out her best effort?

ESTELLE. Not really. I just don't think it works that way.

JULIE. It has always worked for me before. I'm pretty confident I can manage this week.

LEON. Oh, then, you don't really need our prayers anymore?

JULIE. Of course, I need your prayers. What is this? I feel like you are all talking in circles.

ESTELLE. Well, you asked for our prayers. That sounds like you want help from "without." You want us to ask God to help you.

LEON. But in the next breath, you say that you are going to dig deep within yourself for strength, and that you are pretty sure you can handle the week.

VAUGHN. That's right, Julie. I think Estelle is saying that if you have confidence in *yourself*, why do you need God's help?

JULIE. I have to admit that I was thinking in that direction. I wasn't really asking for God's help, was I? Maybe that's why I've been so stressed lately. I act like I want God's help, but I shut Him out and do it my own way.

ESTELLE. I don't think we should depend on *inner* strength. It should be *outer* strength. A power outside ourselves that is all-knowing and all-powerful.

VAUGHN. Yeah, Julie. Look to God for His power for the tasks of this week.

JULIE. Thanks for the lesson in trust, everybody. Now, with God's help, I have every confidence that this week is going to be just fine.

Inner Strength?

As it is written: "There is no one righteous, not even one."

Romans 3:10

I was reading an article about the importance of inner strength in becoming an Olympic athlete. It made me stop and think. Is that biblical? Do Christians look within to stand in the face of difficulty? I couldn't think of a Bible passage that would lead to introspection. I did, on the other hand, think of author Corrie ten Boom's admonition, "Look at the world and be distressed, look at yourself and be depressed, look at Christ and be at rest."

Inner strength seems an oxymoron when viewed from this perspective. The psalmist cries out, "If you, O Lord, kept a record of sins, O Lord, who could stand?"(Psalm 130:3). Inner rottenness leads to inner collapse, not inner strength.

I like to think of "outer" strength. I, a poor miserable sinner, am weak. God, the giver of every good and perfect gift, is strong. "A mighty fortress is our God," says Martin Luther. "Rock of ages, cleft for me, let me hide myself in Thee," says a hymn writer. "I lift up my eyes to the hills—where does my help come from? My help comes from the Lord, the Maker of heaven and earth," proclaims the writer of the 121st psalm.

Sometimes, we take what is a world thought, e.g., inner strength, and make our own interpretation. Many acknowledge that it is the Christ within that makes us strong, but I think we would do well to remember that we are utterly corrupt. I know that in me dwells no good thing, and it is hard to separate the idea of inner strength from even the smallest bit of pride.

The Children of Israel were saved from the poisonous snake bites in the desert by looking up at the bronze snake that God instructed Moses to put on a pole. We, too, need to look to the hills, to the heavens, to the cross for our salvation. "Outer" strength. Honoring and revering an Almighty God who dwells outside of our prideful selves. I'm with Ms. ten Boom. "Look at yourself and be depressed. Look at Christ and be at rest."

Heavenly Father, we confess to You the many times that we do not hand over our daily tasks and problems into Your care, because we like to depend on our own strength. Forgive our attitude of self-sufficiency, for we know that without Your sustaining hand we could not take our next breath. Develop in us an awareness of Your constant care, and help us to look to You for our daily needs. Thank You that You have given us eyes and ears, our reason, and all our senses, and that you still preserve them. Remove our eyes from the pride of self-accomplishment and turn them to You, the Giver of every good and perfect gift. For the eyes of all wait upon You, O Lord, and You give them their food in due season. You open Your hand and satisfy the desires of every living thing. In Jesus' name we pray. Amen.

Here Am I. Send me!

ESTELLE. You know, I wish I had gone into church work when I had the call.

LEON. You had the call?

ESTELLE. I think I did. As a child, my mother and grandmother made sure that I went to a parochial school. I admired my teachers, and I wanted to be just like them. I wanted to teach and to love and care for kids, just like I felt loved and cared for by those Christian teachers.

JULIE. If you wanted to teach and felt called by God, what stopped you?

ESTELLE. Well, for one thing, no one else seemed to think I would be a good teacher. At least no one ever said anything to me about serving God as a teacher. And none of my high school friends were very religious, so they didn't think it was a good idea.

VAUGHN. It's funny you should say that. It made me remember that when I was in high school, my pastor told me he thought I would make a good preacher. Ha. I just laughed it off because, at the time, I was barely even going to church. Football was all I was thinking about.

LEON. This is an interesting conversation. We were just talking about Timothy in Bible class the other day. Timothy, like Estelle, was nurtured in the faith early in his life by his grandmother and mother. And, like Vaughn, he was encouraged by his pastor, Paul, to serve God as a pastor. He was in close fellowship with God and other believers, so, when he was encouraged, he accepted God's call.

JULIE. His faith was strengthened by the faith of others in his life. I know I would really miss the encouragement of my Bible study group.

ESTELLE. You're right, Julie. I was close to God, but I wasn't surrounding myself with other believers who might have encouraged me, so I didn't listen when God called.

VAUGHN. And I had someone encourage me by telling me I would make a good pastor, but I wasn't strong enough in my faith to listen.

JULIE. God gives us all gifts and calls us to use them to serve Him, but we have to stay close to God to keep the flame of faith alive.

LEON. And we need the company of other believers so that we can be encouraged by one another to be ready to answer God's call when it comes.

JULIE. Why don't you volunteer to be a Sunday school teacher, Estelle? They're always looking for good leaders. I think you have a wonderful way with kids.

ESTELLE. Thanks for the encouragement, Julie. I think I will.

Here Am I. Send Me!

Then I heard the voice of the LORD saying, "Whom shall I send? And who will go for us?" And I said, "Here am I. Send me!"

Isaiah 6:8

I don't know how many times we had missionaries visit our church when I was a child, but I remember being captivated by their stories of faraway lands and faraway peoples.

Many brought colorful pictures of cultures very different from my own. Usually, this included pictures of strange-looking men and women worshiping together. We rejoiced that new Christians had received the Good News of salvation through Jesus Christ, and I remember being in awe of the missionaries, those faithful carriers of the gospel.

In response to the Lord's question, "Whom shall I send?" the prophet Isaiah replies in fervent ardor, "Here am I. Send me!" As a child, I wondered, "Would I ever say those words? Could I ever go to a foreign land to tell others about Jesus?"

For many years my pastor husband served a rural congregation. Being a "city girl" moving out to the country was quite a change for me. I sometimes felt like I had had been asked to go to a foreign land, but I was young and willing to go wherever God sent me. Isaiah, too, was expressing his willingness to go wherever God assigned him to go, but today, as I was reading these verses from Isaiah, it occurred to me that there was more to the story than that. It was not just a matter of where Isaiah was to be sent, but to whom he was sent.

God asks for someone to send on a mission. Isaiah volunteers. And then God sends him to be a messenger to people who will: "Be ever hearing, but never understanding" (Isaiah 6:9).

God's plan is that Isaiah is to bring God's message to a people who are "never" going to understand? And, says God, the message he is to preach will actually serve to harden the hearts of the hearers. This sounds like a thankless task, at best.

Sometimes God calls us to seemingly thankless tasks: we are to be patient under a harsh and thoughtless boss or we are at home, tired and discouraged from caring for small children. Perhaps we teach school but cannot in any way mention to the children under our care anything about a God who loves them or perhaps we long to change the world but instead stay home to care for an ailing parent. Maybe we want to have a family that worships God together, but our marriage is in shambles. Maybe we go to the seminary to be a pastor and leave, eager to set the world afire for Jesus, and are sent to a small church in a small community that fears change or perhaps we have a handicapped child whose care leaves us drained at the end of each day.

Staying faithful in these situations is not what we usually think of when we say to God, "Send me!" Isaiah must have been at least a little surprised at his assignment. He is still willing, though, because his next response is not a refusal. Instead he asks, "For how long, O Lord?"

God's answer? "Until the cities lie ruined and without inhabitant" (Isaiah 6:11). Actually, the nation is going to be destroyed right down to a few stumps out of which it would one day grow again. This was surely not the answer for which Isaiah was looking.

God's plans are so far-reaching that we are unable to see the whole picture. We often don't understand our part in the big design. Yet God has purpose for our lives, and He wants to hear us say, "Here am I. Send me!" And then He wants us to go, uncomplaining, to do His will. It is called obedience.

"Through him and for his name's sake, we received grace and apostleship to call people from among all the Gentiles to the obedience that comes by faith" (Romans 1: 5).

By faith, we respond to God's call, just as Isaiah did. And, by faith, we serve where God sends us, even if the task seems futile. Especially if the task seems futile.

Dear Father in Heaven, we praise You this day for the example of faithful and willing men, such as the prophet Isaiah. Forgive us for the many times we do not want to go where You call us to go and for the times we rebel at the tasks You give us to do. Remind us that we cannot fully see Your great plan of salvation, nor our part in it. As we put our trust in Your strength, give us the obedience that comes by faith and stirs our hearts to cry, "Here am I. Send me!" We ask in Jesus' name. Amen.

He is Risen, Indeed

LEON. Happy Easter, everyone!

DANNY. Yeah, Happy Easter! I love holidays.

LISA. We usually have a bittersweet celebration at Easter time.

ALAN. Yeah. Three years ago my sister's five-year-old, Angie, was killed in a car accident coming home from the family get-together at our house.

LISA. I'll never forget that phone call.

ESTELLE. That's so sad.

DANNY. I'll bet that kind of ruins Easter for your family.

LISA. Actually, it has made this one of our most important holidays.

ALAN. We could never have gotten through that time without the sure promise that Angie was safe in heaven with Jesus.

LEON. That is the important message of Easter. Because He is risen, we, too, will rise and live with Him in heaven.

DANNY. I think heaven will be fun.

LISA. It helps us a lot to think of Angie having a great time in heaven. It helps to picture how happy she is snuggled in Jesus' loving arms.

ESTELLE. You know, I've always thought of Jesus' death and resurrection as being an important part of my faith, but really it's *the* most important part, isn't it?

LEON. Exactly right, Estelle.

ALAN. And we are all looking forward to seeing Angie in heaven.

DANNY. He is risen!

EVERYONE. He is risen, indeed. Alleluia!

He is Risen, Indeed

If there is no resurrection of the dead, then not even Christ has been raised. And if Christ has not been raised, our preaching is useless and so is your faith.

1 Corinthians 15:13–14

Jesus' resurrection is the central truth of all Christianity. Sometimes we forget that. Yet, as St. Paul points out, either it is true or the whole thing collapses and our faith is in vain.

But it is true, as evidenced by the rapid growth of the church after Pentecost. The Christians of that day had first-hand knowledge of the resurrection. Many personally knew someone who had seen Jesus' dead body being taken down from the cross and who had also seen His risen body during one of His many appearances after he rose from the dead.

It is wonderful to know that death could not hold the Son of God. It is even more wonderful to learn that because Christ defeated death, we, too, will rise. Have you ever thought how freeing it is to live without the fear of death? Only in Christ are we able to face our future with confidence. To be sure, death is the final enemy, but a defeated enemy nonetheless.

The story is told of Adolph Hitler lamenting the fact that Christians in Germany were resisting the ideology of the Third Reich.

"What we need is a new religion for the people," he said. "Any ideas?" he asked of his staff.

"That's easy," one of his officers responded. "All we have to do is find someone who can die and come back to life again."

Satan has tried over the centuries and throughout the world to come up with a different religion, but he, like Hitler, cannot fool the faithful follower of Christ. What sets Christianity apart from any other religion is Easter: the promise that Christ's victory over death is our own, not earned, but a gift of God.

For God so loved the world that He gave his one and only Son, that whoever believes in him shall not perish but have eternal life.

John 3:16

So have a happy Easter, resting in the sure promise of Eternal Life.

Heavenly Father, today we celebrate the fulfillment of Your promise to send a Savior for the world. Down through the centuries men longed for this day. We lift up Your Holy name in praise for the wondrous gift of salvation. You showed Your great love for us through the suffering and death of Your only Son and have granted us the power to share in His resurrection; His great victory over death. Because He lives, we, too, will rise. We can now say, with Job, "I know that my Redeemer lives, and that in the end he will stand upon the earth. And after my skin is destroyed, yet in my flesh I will see God; I myself will see him with my own eyes—I, and not another" (Job 19:25–27a). He is risen, indeed. Alleluia. Amen.

Pressing On Toward the Goal

JULIE. Usually I ignore those quiz things in magazines, but last week I found one that really made me think.

VAUGHN. I hate the ones that tell you what you are good at and what you are bad at. It mostly turns out that I am not good at anything.

LEON. Remember those tests in school that tried to steer you toward a certain vocation? When I got my results back, it said that I should be a shepherd!

ESTELLE. That's hilarious, Leon. I think most of those assessment tests are pretty lame, so what caught your interest in this one, Julie?

JULIE. Well, first, it made you write down ten goals for your life: how much money you wanted to be earning ten years from now, what size house you wanted, places you would like to vacation—things like that.

LEON. They say written goals are very powerful.

JULIE. But then they had you write out ten things that were most important to you. Things like your relationship with Jesus, family, friends, free time—at least those were what was on my list.

ESTELLE. So you liked that it made you think ahead a little?

JULIE. Not that, exactly. Instead, it asked us to seriously consider whether or not our goals matched our values. I was shocked to find that wanting a bigger house did not lead to more free time for Bible study or prayer or time to spend with family and friends, all of which were listed as my top values.

VAUGHN. I get it. If you wanted the big house, you had to give up time in order to get the bigger paycheck to pay for the house.

LEON. I think St. Paul had a good hold on that principle, Julie. He had set goals early in his life. He wanted a good education, a place of high position among his peers, and a reputation for being zealous. But when he found Christ, he knew that his values no longer fit his goals.

ESTELLE. He left behind everything he used to be in order to pursue his faith in Christ.

JULIE. I should go back to that quiz and see how many of my goals have little to do with having a relationship with Christ. After all, that was at the top of my values list.

ESTELLE. Hey, Julie. Do you mind if I borrow that quiz?

Pressing on Toward the Goal

Dear friends, I urge you, as aliens and strangers in the world, to abstain from sinful desires, which war against your soul.

1 Peter 2:11

Have you ever heard the saying, "Begin with the end in mind"? This is often quoted in books about setting goals and having big plans for your life. It is the reason large and small companies, even churches, develop mission statements. The idea is that if we know where we are headed, we will have a basis for making the many decisions that will confront us on the way to our goals.

St. Peter gives us similar advice. He calls us aliens and strangers. The implied message is that we are just journeying through this world on our way to our real destination— heaven. Knowing this makes our earthly journey different from those who do not know Christ and His salvation.

Those who see this life as "all there is" behave differently when confronted by temptation than those who have heaven as a higher goal. King Solomon decried the futility of this life. The richest and wisest man who ever lived found nothing that satisfied, and he had tried it all. "Meaningless!

Meaningless!" says the teacher. "Everything is meaningless!" (Ecclesiastes 12:8).

Taken from this perspective, Peter's admonition "to abstain from sinful desires, which war against your soul" (1 Peter 2:11) makes perfect sense. Why give in to those things that do not satisfy, especially when those things could cause us to lose the battle and die before we make it safely home? After all, we are only strangers and sojourners here.

I have heard the saying, "When in Rome, do as the Romans do," but that is the world's wisdom. St. Peter tells us earlier in this chapter, in verse 9, "But you are a chosen people, a royal priesthood, a holy nation, a people belonging to God, that you may declare the praises of Him who called you out of darkness into His wonderful light" (1 Peter 2:9). We are to be in the world, but not of the world, declaring to those in darkness the news of something far, far better.

So let us begin with heaven in mind and "abstain from sinful desires that war against [our] soul[s]"(1 Peter 2:11). Then, as we follow Christ and accept His forgiveness, we are given a glimpse of heaven right here and now, making our sojourn on earth special, as well.

Heavenly Father, we thank and praise You that You have given us a Savior. Now we no longer fear death; rather, we look forward to our citizenship in heaven. As we journey through the perils of this life, help us to shun all things that would cause us to take our eyes off the prize of living with You in heaven. Thank

You for the many blessings of this life, as well as the promise of the life to come. "Teach us to number our days aright, that we may gain a heart of wisdom" (Psalm 90:12). Help us to remain Your servants now and into eternity. In Jesus' name we pray. Amen.

Abba, Father

VAUGHN. Happy Father's Day, Leon and Alan. I'm thinking about my dad today and how grateful I am for his influence in my life.

LEON. My dad was a great guy. He had a wonderful sense of humor. I can still hear his laugh when he heard a good joke.

ALAN. My dad taught me how to do so many of the things I do today. I can fix about anything around the house, and I've been changing the oil in my car and doing my own tune-ups ever since I had my first car. Dad taught me all that stuff.

JULIE. My dad came to every ballgame, every choir concert, every dance recital, and every play I was ever in. He never missed a thing.

ESTELLE. My father was always busy. He rarely ate with us because of his work. He missed most of my plays, never came to any of my softball games and, even though I sat first chair in the clarinet section for four years of high school, I don't think he ever came to a band concert.

ALAN. It doesn't sound like he took his parenting seriously.

JULIE. I don't think I would have liked that.

VAUGHN. I hope I'm not that kind of dad to my kids.

LEON. Do you resent it, Estelle?

ESTELLE. Oh, no! I forgot to tell you what he *did* do. He went to church with us every Sunday. He said our prayers with us before bed on the nights he was home. He made sure we knew that he loved us and that we knew that Jesus loved us. I guess I never much noticed the things he *didn't* do.

VAUGHN. Wow, Estelle. He did all the most important stuff, even though he was busy. I think I *would* like to be a dad like that.

Abba, Father

Because you are sons, God sent the Spirit of his Son into our hearts, the Spirit who calls out, "*Abba*, Father." So you are no longer a slave, but a son; and since you are a son, God has made you also an heir."

Galatians 4:6, 7

There are children of every generation who, for one reason or another, never know their fathers. Psychologists tell us this leaves a hole in peoples' lives that is not easily filled. Fathers are part of God's plan, but when sin entered the world, many of God's plans became spoiled. Now we have death and war, so some fathers die before their children know them. Sexual liaisons produce children whom many fathers never acknowledge. Divorce and separation take fathers out of the home and, in all this, it is the children who suffer most.

Did you know that all of us entered this world not knowing our Heavenly Father? Those of us with Christian parents were introduced to Him at an early age. Others of us found our Father at a later date. But the sad thing is that there are still many children of God who do not know their Father in Heaven. And it leaves a void. Most do not realize what it is that is missing from their lives. But the void remains.

God seeks us out, even when we do not seek Him. "Because you are sons," says St. Paul, "God sent the Spirit of His Son into our hearts" (Galatians 4:6). To be sure, we can reject that Spirit, and many do. But when we believe that Jesus has broken down the wall of sin that separates us from God, the Spirit causes us to call out, "Abba, Father."

I know people who have sought to locate the children they had put up for adoption as infants. The circumstances have changed and the child that could not be raised by his or her parent is now longed for by that very mom and/or dad. Sometimes these parents are able to find and meet the son or daughter they had once given up to others. You can imagine their joy when the child is found.

God, too, longs to bring us back into a relationship with Him. He wants to fill the void in our hearts with an unconditional and overflowing love. When Satan has control of us, we are slaves to him, whether we know it or not. But, St. Paul tells us, when we let the Spirit of Christ into our hearts, we are no longer slaves, but sons and heirs. Then we call out "Abba, Father," and it is our Father's good pleasure to call us His children and to integrate us fully into His family.

Have you ever stopped to consider how rich is the God of the universe? Well, Psalm 50:12 says, "If I were hungry I would not tell you, for the world is mine, and all that is in it." You have a very wealthy Father, and He is glad to make you an heir of that wealth, not just with riches that feed the body, but riches that feed the soul and mind as well.

The first prayer I learned from my parents, who were of German heritage, was, "Abba, lieber Vater. Amen." It translates, "Father, dear Father. Amen." It is a wonderful thing to know your Father and to be claimed by Him as both child and heir.

"Abba, Father!" We approach Thee
In our Savior's precious Name;
We, Thy children, here assembled,
Now Thy promised blessing claim;
From our sins His blood hath washed us,
'Tis through Him our souls draw nigh,
And Thy Spirit, too, hath taught us,
"Abba, Father," thus to cry. Amen.

James G. Deck (1807–1884)

Foolish to the Wise

VAUGHN. You want to hear something pretty stupid?

LEON. I'm always up for a stupid story, Vaughn.

VAUGHN. Well, I went to ask my neighbor if I could borrow his lawnmower, and he said he couldn't loan it to me because he had had pancakes for breakfast.

DANNY. That is pretty stupid.

VAUGHN. And, besides that, he said it wouldn't work out for me to use his mower because his wife had gone shopping.

JULIE. What kind of an excuse is that?

VAUGHN. I asked him that very question, and he said, "Really, when you don't want to loan out your lawnmower, any old excuse will do."

ESTELLE. Now that is a very true statement. What seemed foolish at first was actually very wise.

DANNY. I think I'm going to get a major in wisdom when I go to college.

JULIE. Let me know when you find a school that teaches that. I'm afraid you are going to have to search far and wide to find a place to study wisdom.

LEON. Not exactly true, Julie. The place to learn wisdom is as close as picking up your Bible, and a good start would be turning to Proverbs.

ESTELLE. "The fear of the Lord is the beginning of wisdom," right, Leon?

LEON. Right, Estelle.

Foolish to the Wise

The stone the builders rejected has become the capstone; the LORD has done this, and it is marvelous in our eyes. This is the day the LORD has made; let us rejoice and be glad in it.

Psalm 118:22–24

People with handicaps experience the world's rejection in many ways. They have been referred to as a "burden" on society. Frequently, doctors use amniocenteses, a procedure that can identify medical conditions of a baby still in the womb. Often, based on the test results, doctors counsel parents to abort a less-than-perfect child.

But man's judgment is flawed when it comes to things of true value. God's way of measuring worth is far different from our own. God does marvelous things. He creates people of all shapes, sizes, and abilities. And so, the psalmist tells us, each day we rise up and say, "This is the day the Lord has made, let us rejoice and be glad in it" (Psalm 118:24).

For many years our family spent a week at Camp Omega in southern Minnesota during developmentally disabled week. These grown, yet childlike, campers were a delight. They knew how to rejoice in each day.

We would say, "It's time for breakfast."

"Yea!" they would shout.

"It's time to clear the tables."

"Yea!" they would shout.

"It's time for Bible Study."

"Yea!" they would shout.

"It's FOB (feet on bunk) time."

"Yea!" we would hear once again.

"It's time to sing. It's time to swim. It's time to take a shower."

"Yea! Yea! Yea!" was the cheerful response.

"It's time for bed."

"Yea!" we all would shout.

First Corinthians 1:27 says that God chose the foolish things of the world to shame the wise, and He chose the weak things of the world to shame the strong. When I think of the faith with which those mentally challenged campers moved through the day, I am indeed shamed. Many days, instead of rejoicing, I am a downright complainer.

When is the last time you shouted, "Yea!" at every step of your day? If it is true, and it is, that "in all things God works for the good of those who love him, who have been called according to his purpose" (Romans 8:28), than "Yea!" should be our invariable response as well.

So, to all you wise, strong, and healthy people out there, the campers from Camp Omega's mentally challenged week want to remind you:

This is the day, (echo),
That the Lord has made, (echo)
We will rejoice, (echo)
And be glad in it! (echo)
This is the day that the Lord has made,
We will rejoice and be glad in it!
This is the day, (echo)
That the Lord has made.

Yea!

I Wait for the Lord

VAUGHN. Hello, everyone. (*Sees Dixie*) Oh, and who are you?

DIXIE. I'm Dixie. The kids and I just joined here. That Pastor Braun sure doesn't give up, does he? I never had so many visits from a preacher before. Anyway, it was easier to come to church than tell him no, so here we are.

LEON. Dixie, huh? Are you from the South?

DIXIE. No. My dad works for that company that makes those little paper cups, you know, so Dixie it was for me.

LEON. Welcome, Dixie. It's nice to have you here.

DIXIE. Thanks.

ESTELLE. I've been dying to tell all of you what happened at this wedding I went to yesterday. They almost ran out of food.

DIXIE. We wouldn't have run out of food at my wedding, but we almost ran out of a bride and groom. I wasn't sure which one of us wanted to be a no-show more. Actually, one of us probably should have run out.

Everyone pauses to look at Dixie. No one knows how to respond, so Estelle goes back to her story.

ESTELLE. Well, anyway, those of us near the food table just sat and prayed that God would let there be enough food to make it through to the last guest.

VAUGHN. Well, did they make it?

ESTELLE. Barely, but they made it.

LEON. Just like in the Bible.

DANNY. I know that one: the Wedding at Cana.

DIXIE. What, they ran out of food in the Bible?

LEON. Actually, they ran out of wine at a wedding in the Bible.

DIXIE. And then to tell everybody by putting it in the Bible! How embarrassing! Oh, man, I would have died.

ESTELLE. Well, they didn't run out. Jesus turned water into wine. Actually that was the first miracle He did.

LEON. That must have been a relief to his mother.

DANNY. What, did she like wine that much?

VAUGHN. I think Leon means that Mary went to Jesus and asked Him to do something about the problem. After that, she just had to wait and have faith that He would help.

ESTELLE. The disciples, too, had been waiting, looking for a sign that this was the Messiah. This miracle must have been an answer to their prayers, as well.

DANNY. A lot of times I have to wait for an answer, but I know that Jesus loves me. I guess waiting's not so bad when you know you'll receive an answer eventually. Even the disciples did it.

I Wait for the Lord

I wait for the LORD, my soul waits, and in His word I put my hope. My soul waits for the LORD more than watchmen wait for the morning, more than watchmen wait for the morning.

Psalm 130:5–6

Psalm 130:6 has special meaning for me. I worked "nights" for more than ten years. The sweetest sound to those of us on what they often call the "graveyard shift" is the singing of birds, just as the dawn is breaking. That sound promises relief. Someone is soon going to step off the elevator and take over. Our duty done, we will head home for some longed-for sleep.

In Hebrew poetry the thought in the first half of the verse is often rephrased in the second half of the verse. It is interesting that, in this verse, the thought is repeated verbatim. Do you think that perhaps the psalmist had experienced night duty? That perhaps he remembered how hard it is to stay awake when everyone around him is sound asleep?

In this case, longing for the morning is synonymous with longing for relief. The watchmen look forward to handing off all the cares and pressures that have been placed under their responsibility. You and I are weighed down by many trials as well. They are the kinds of things that keep us awake at night: money worries, concern for our children or our marriage, war, terror attacks, natural disasters. You name yours. I know mine.

On nights like that I cling to the phrase, "My soul waits, and in his word I put my hope" (Psalm 130:5). Sometimes we do have to wait for God to answer. The night can seem long. My father, who had emphysema, would lie awake at night, unable to sleep, always conscious of his next effortful breath. He used to tell us that in the morning the clock went back to "honest" time, when each minute seemed like a minute, not an hour.

But for us Christians there is hope. Just as the watchman knows the morning will come, for God promises that as long as the earth remains the sun will continue to rise and fall on schedule, so do we know that God will come to our rescue. We are not in this alone. Solving our problems may seem beyond our abilities, but God can handle them.

If you are going through a hard time right now, the Psalmist has good advice. Wait and hope in the Lord. Waiting is not usually our strong suit, but waiting with hope is different.

Remember the agony of waiting for Christmas as kids? And yet, the high state of excitement it produced? That's the kind of waiting the Psalmist is talking about. Instead of viewing life as an endless parade of problems, we are given the opportunity to view it as an endless opportunity to be surprised by God.

Hope asks, "I wonder how God will bless me in this situation," or "I wonder if this is the day I find out God's plan for me now."

Faith says, "I'll bet God has something wonderful in store for me."

And lo and behold waiting turns to anticipation.

Isn't the Christian life exciting?

Dear Heavenly Father, sometimes life is hard. The trials of this world remind us of how much more perfect our life will be with You in heaven. For now, though, we groan under the weight of the burdens we bear. Often in the night we are tired and afraid and we long for relief. Reassure us that the problems that seem unsolvable from our viewpoint are never too big for You. We now give these struggles to You, placing them into Your loving care, knowing that Your strength is made perfect in our weakness, for our hope is in You. We ask in Jesus' name. Amen.

Knowing God

LEON. Hey, have any of you seen the movie *Titanic?* I saw it last night and I think it's going to be a big hit.

VAUGHN. Well, you got the big hit part right, but that movie has been around for years, Leon.

LEON. Next week, I'm going to see *My Big Fat Greek Wedding.* It's supposed to be good, too.

ESTELLE. I think we have all seen that one as well, Leon. Where are you getting your information? You are usually pretty up to date on things like this.

JULIE. Hey, Leon. You want a hot tip? See *(Insert the name of a current blockbuster film.)*

LEON. Is that a movie?

VAUGHN. It's a great movie. Everybody's talking about it. It's brand new, and it's doing well in the theatres right now.

LEON. Thanks for telling me, Vaughn.

ESTELLE. You know, I was thinking. What if no one had told me about Jesus?

JULIE. I see what you're getting at. The message of God's love for us through Jesus' death and resurrection has been around a long time.

VAUGHN. But if you were out of the loop, like Leon has been on the movie scene, you might not have heard the good news of salvation.

JULIE. That would be awful. I think everybody already knows about Jesus, don't they?

ESTELLE. I don't think they do, Julie. If Leon, who is usually very up to date about current events, could be so behind in something as run of the mill as the movie scene, then I'll bet there are people who don't know about Jesus either.

VAUGHN. How do they know unless somebody tells them? Just to be sure everybody's heard, we'd better spread the word.

Knowing God

Who has believed our message and to whom has the
arm of the LORD been revealed?

Isaiah 53:1

Interesting questions. I think I would have reversed the order,
asking, "To whom has the arm of the Lord been revealed?"
And then, following with the question, "Okay, now who has
believed what the arm of the Lord has revealed?" Learn about
God first, then decide to believe.

However, knowing that the Old Testament writers often
stated their thoughts in parallel lines, restating them, if you
will, I think Isaiah is telling us that God reveals Himself to
those who believe. He means God doesn't uncover His goodness and majesty in the face of unbelief. There is a verse in the
New Testament where Jesus cautions us about throwing pearls
to swine. Perhaps this would be a case of doing just that.

It makes sense. Jesus says, "I am the good shepherd;
I know my sheep and my sheep know me" (John 10:14).
The believer recognizes the voice of the shepherd, the non-
believer does not. Why not? He doesn't know the shepherd.
Nothing about God is known to him.

This Isaiah passage is found quoted in Romans 10:16:
"But not all the Israelites accepted the good news. For Isaiah

says, 'Lord, who has believed our message?'" The next verse continues, "Consequently, faith comes from hearing the message, and the message is heard through the word of Christ" (Romans 10:17). The problem is, the message is not always accepted.

God reveals Himself to the believer—the one who does accept the message. Until faith was worked in our hearts through hearing about God's love for us through Jesus Christ, we did not know that God is love. We did not know that all things work together for our good. We did not know that God had plans for us. We didn't get it.

And neither does the unbeliever. He just doesn't get it. And guess what that means for you and for me? We need to get out the message of the Gospel. Our non-Christian friends are not going to come to faith through communing with nature. They are not going to see our good works and come to faith. They are unlikely to seek out a church hoping to hear of Christ's love. They do not know the Shepherd's voice. Faith comes through hearing the message of salvation through the words of Jesus Christ. And they need to hear those words from us.

And when, through the power of the Holy Spirit, they do indeed believe the message, God will reveal Himself to them in a way they never before understood. And they will be able to call Him Father and know His loving care.

Heavenly Father, we know that You would have all men to be saved and come to the knowledge of the truth. You have shown us that this knowledge comes only through the good news of Your Son, Jesus Christ. Thank You for revealing Yourself to us, and keep us ever-mindful of the many who live in unbelief, who know nothing of Your love. Help us to be ready with the saving Gospel on our lips, that others, too, may know You in all our glory. We ask in Jesus' name. Amen.

Jesus Loves the Little Children!

VAUGHN. Good morning, everyone. I feel great. Tell me your ills and woes. Nothing seems too big to handle today.

LEON. I used to have days like that once.

DANNY. You're like a superhero, Vaughn.

ESTELLE. It's nice to feel in control for once.

JULIE. I used to feel that way too, Estelle, but now I'm not convinced I like feeling so sure of myself all the time.

VAUGHN. You'd rather feel weak and insignificant? I've had those days and I don't think I like them very much.

JULIE. Well, weak and insignificant worked for me last week.

LEON. What do you mean it worked for you?

JULIE. Well, my good friend Lisa came over last Thursday and was crying about a fight she had with her sister. She knows how much I like to analyze things and look at all angles for possible solutions.

ESTELLE. Me too. I can always think of great ways to solve other people's problems.

LEON. So, did you get that particular problem sorted out for her?

JULIE. The fact is, I was so tired I couldn't even sort my own day out, so I said, "Lisa, let's just pray about this. God will know best how to work this out. He's a God of love, so He'll know what to do." So we just prayed about it and Lisa went home feeling a lot better.

DANNY. See, Lisa was smart to come to you. You do know how to help.

JULIE. But don't you see? It was only because I was too tired to come up with all my usual solutions that we thought to cast our cares on the One who cares for us.

LEON. It was your weakness that made you strong.

VAUGHN. Well, then, I still feel great today, but any problem that comes along, I'll turn over to God. Then my puny solutions won't block His strong ones.

ESTELLE. That's a great plan, Vaughn. When we turn to God for help, we respond with His wisdom and understanding. Our weak ideas are replaced by His all-knowing, all-loving response to our needs.

Jesus Loves the Little Children!

But the fruit of the Spirit is love, joy, peace, patience, kindness, goodness, faithfulness, gentleness, and self-control. Against such things there is no law.

Galatians 5:22

As a young mother of three boys I was often at the end of my rope. One morning, when I had had enough of the kids running wildly through the house, I snagged my oldest child, Philip, age three at the time, and gave him a whack on the bottom.

Philip looked at me with astonishment and said, with tears in his eyes, "Mother! Jesus *loves* the little children!"

I knew when I grabbed him that I was intent on getting order my way, not God's way. But I hadn't, until that moment, realized that in my son's eyes, I was a reflection of God's love toward him. I had told my son about God's love and how we are then able to love others in return, but my actions did not match my words.

God hates sin, but He doesn't smack us on the seat of our pants when we disobey. I deserved a spanking of my own just then. Instead, I got a potent lesson in kindness "from the mouth of babes."

If we find ourselves yelling often at our children, our spouses, our coworkers, or all of the above, we might want to take a step back from berating these children of God and remember that "Jesus *loves* the little children" (even the big ones). And if they know we are Christians, they are going to learn what they know about God by observing us.

That is a little scary, right? Well, there is hope for us. St. Paul says, "The fruit of the Spirit is love, joy, peace, patience, kindness, goodness, faithful, gentleness, self control." I knew I had lost it on all counts in my parenting that morning, for out of a sinful heart comes all sorts of evil; unless, of course, we have given control of that heart to Jesus.

So, the next time we are about to "lose it," it would be good for us to stop and ask for *God's* kindness to show through to the source of our frustration. We need to let the love of Christ live in us richly so that His Spirit's response becomes ours: love, joy, peace, patience, kindness.

Then not only will others see Christ in us, we will know that He dwells there as well. As we give our hearts to Jesus, others will see, as my young son, Philip, tearfully reminded me, "Jesus *loves* the little children!"

> *O Jesus, King most wonderful*
> *Thou Conqueror renowned,*
> *Thou Sweetest most ineffable,*
> *In whom all joys are found!*
> *When once Thou visitest the heart,*

The truth begins to shine,
Then earthly vanities depart,
Then kindles love divine.
Thee may our tongues forever bless,
Thee may we love alone,
And ever in our lives express
The image of Thine own!

Unknown author, twelfth century;
translated by Edward Caswall, 1848

Bless This House

LEON. You know, my wife and I have a wedding anniversary coming in the next couple of months, and I've been thinking back to that time.

JULIE. Wedding plans. Oh, I just loved all the planning and dreaming. Shopping for my wedding dress and deciding what the attendants would wear, picking out the cake and choosing flowers. It was great.

DANNY. That sounds more like a nightmare to me. It seems like too much work, too many decisions to make.

VAUGHN. That's the part you were remembering, Leon?

LEON. Not really. I remember that busy time too, Julie, and it's more fun than you think, Danny. But what I was remembering was how carefully we selected the overall theme for our Bible readings. We wanted to start off on the right foot.

ESTELLE. A theme for the wedding, or a theme for your marriage?

LEON. That's a good point, Estelle. We wanted a theme for our marriage, so we took our motto from the words of Joshua that we just read in the Old Testament lesson today:

"Decide you this day whom you will serve. But as for me and my house, we will serve the Lord."

JULIE. Well, how have you done so far?

LEON. That's what I asked myself recently. I realized the importance of renewing those promises daily because it sure is easy to forget what we started out to do.

ESTELLE. We should all have that as our theme. As for me and my house, we will serve the Lord.

DANNY. I'm willing to have that as my theme, but I don't see how I can do that each day.

VAUGHN. First of all, it would be important to start and end each day with prayer, Danny. We sin daily and need to ask for forgiveness daily. We would also need to begin every day with a new resolve to serve the Lord with all our hearts and put our faith and trust in Him.

JULIE. I'll bet we'd be amazed at the difference that would make in our lives. Okay, as for me and my house, we will serve the Lord.

Bless This House

Sometimes a song or hymn can have special meaning in your life. One of the hymns sung at our wedding offered some wonderful principles for marriage and family that I ponder often. The hymn is: *Oh Blest the House* by Christoph C. L. von Pfeil (1712–1784).

Verse 1:

Oh blest the house, whate're befall, where Jesus Christ is all in all.
Yea, if He were not dwelling there, how dark, and poor, and void it were!

Are things falling apart at your place? Is every day an effort? Is your home dark and poor and void? All that changes when Jesus becomes the center. Where Jesus dwells, nothing is dark and poor. French philosopher and physicist Blaise Pascal said that within the heart of every man is a God-shaped void that cannot be filled by created things. Material things could never fill our house with warmth and joy. Those blessings are found only in homes where "Jesus Christ is all in all."

Verse 2:

> Oh, blest that house where faith ye find and all
> within have set their mind
> To trust their God and serve Him still and do
> in all His holy will!

This was our desire right from the beginning of our marriage. Both our parents had set faithful examples for us. Also, I remember a plaque we received as a wedding gift that read "Christ is the head this house; the unseen guest at every meal; the silent listener to every conversation." We wanted that to set the tone for our home. Of course we often failed to place God first, but we would ask forgiveness and begin again. The goal remained. You may not have had parents who provided good examples for Christian living, but you can look to Christian books and follow Christian mentors to help you make this your goal as well. Then *you* become the couple that models this for others.

Verse 3:

> Oh blest the parents who give heed unto their
> children's foremost need,
> And weary not of care or cost! May none to
> them and heaven be lost!

We all love our children. We would do about anything for them. So, do we give heed to their "foremost need"? Is knowing Jesus the top priority in our homes? Sunday morning was our family's time to worship. At our house that meant no sports events scheduled on Sunday mornings, no camping trips that excluded Sunday worship, no travel to other cities or towns without locating a church to attend. Family devotions were a central part of what we were about each day. Again, there were periods when we failed to do this. Still, each time we asked for forgiveness and began again. Do these practices seem burdensome? Not if they provide a way to your children's salvation; not if it meets their "foremost need."

Verse 4:

> Blest such a house it prospers well, in peace
> and joy the parents dwell,
> And in their children's lot is shone how richly
> God can bless His own.

I occasionally watch the TV show where a distressed family calls in a professional nanny to help them change some extremely poor dynamics between parents and children. I don't identify. I had faithful parents and have come to realize that many of my life's blessings have come as a result of their faithfulness. The hymn says that "in their children's lot is shown, how richly God can bless His own." One of those blessings was experiencing a sense of peace and joy in our home.

That has been true of my life, and I want that blessing to spill over into the lives of my children, and their children, and even the children yet to be born. And that can only happen if my children tell their children, and their children tell theirs. I know how thin the thread of faith can become if it is not woven tightly into a family's life. Have you ever considered that how we raise our children might affect the outcome of our great-grandchildren's salvation?

Verse 5:
> Then here will I and mine today
> a solemn covenant make and say:
> Though all the world forsake Thy Word,
> I and my house will serve the Lord!

When Christ is all and all in our homes, faith flourishes and forgiveness flows. When we place our family's care into the hands of God, we no longer fear the task of living in an evil world. Our Heavenly Father lovingly helps us navigate such a world, and we even find peace and joy on the journey. "But as for me and my household, we will serve the Lord" (Joshua 1:5). Decide today that Jesus will be "all in all" in your home. He will do the rest.

Dear Heavenly Father, You instituted marriage and placed each of us in families. We thank You for the gift of family. May You be "all in all" in our homes. Set our hearts to serve You all the days of our lives. Help us not to grow weary in the task of bringing our children to saving faith in Jesus Christ, that we, thereby, meet their foremost need and will have the joy of seeing them in heaven. Help us to say, "Though all the world forsake Thy Word, I and my house will serve the Lord." We pray all this in Jesus' name. Amen.

Pray for Workers

LEON. Good morning, everyone. Are any of you going to help with the church's neighborhood project next Saturday?

DIXIE. What's the neighborhood project?

ESTELLE. Pastor is asking us all to use our gifts in an outreach program. We are going to reach out to others right here in our own neighborhood.

VAUGHN. I'm coordinating the teens. We're offering to do odd jobs for the elderly. We'll probably clean up a few yards, maybe change oil in a few cars—that kind of stuff.

LEON. Well, I heard there's a group going out into the neighborhood to visit with new people in the community to tell them about our church. I think I can make a few calls. I love meeting new people.

DANNY. My mom volunteered to help the little kids do crafts and play games while their parents do other stuff. Next, she volunteered me to help her. I'm supposed to help with games.

ESTELLE. I offered to teach a young women's Bible study while their children are in their activities.

DIXIE. Boy, you are a multitalented group.

DANNY. What are you going to do, Dixie?

DIXIE. Me? I don't have any talent. I'm sure no one will miss me if I didn't show up.

ESTELLE. Of course we'll miss you, Dixie; you're part of the body of Christ.

VAUGHN. Yeah, we don't want to be working on Saturday with any missing body parts, do we?

DANNY. I don't get what you mean.

VAUGHN. The Bible says we are all parts of one body and that each Christian is given a role to make the body function properly.

LEON. Maybe that's why we Christians don't reach out to the community as effectively as we'd like—there are too many missing body parts.

DANNY. Come on, Dixie. We need you.

DIXIE. I guess I could help serve snacks. I saw that was one of the jobs listed. But that's all I would be good for.

DANNY. That's all? What do you mean that's all? We basically come for the snacks, Dixie.

LEON. We really need you, Dixie. Without food the whole body would starve.

Pray for Workers

Then he said to his disciples, "The harvest is plentiful but the workers are few. Ask the LORD of the harvest, therefore, to send out workers into his harvest field."

Matthew 9:37–38

I remember a friend telling me about being a member of an organization in a small community. She and her husband were transplants into the area, and everyone was aware that they did not really "belong." When the organization to which she belonged was getting ready to plan the election of new officers, someone immediately nominated my friend, along with two "regulars," to be on the nominating committee. They sensed that she might be willing to run for office, so they made sure she was unable to vie for a position. Instead, she would be relegated to looking for candidates. She was pretty impressed by their cleverness, but also found out exactly where she stood in that community—on the outside looking in.

Do you think Jesus' disciples might have felt some of this same "rejection"? They were going through the villages with Jesus as He was teaching and preaching, when Jesus points out the need for workers But, instead of giving them the directive to help remedy this lack, He asks them, in essence, to be on the nominating committee. "Ask the Lord of the harvest, therefore, to send out workers into his harvest field."

For some, this would have been a relief. They would be glad to stay home and pray. Sometimes being on the nominating committee is a good, safe place to be when you do not want to have your name placed on the ballot. For those willing to serve, it was humbling to think that others might be asked; that God might not have them in mind for the position.

I often wondered about the disciples' reaction to Jesus' words. It almost seems a slap in the face. The Bible doesn't tell us what their response was, but in the very next verse of the Bible, Matthew 10:1, we find Jesus sending out the twelve disciples to proclaim the good news of the Messiah to the Jews.

So the next time you are relieved by the idea that you can stay home and pray for workers, just remember that those who were asked to pray were the very ones God chose to send!

Lord of the living harvest
That whitens on the plain,
Where angels soon shall gather
Their sheaves of golden grain,
Accept these hands to labor,
These hearts to trust and love,
And with them ever hasten
Your kingdom from above.

John S.B. Monsell (1811–1875)

No Longer Faithless

ESTELLE. I just love summer.

DANNY. Me, too. No school.

VAUGHN. I love the warm weather, too, Estelle.

ESTELLE. It's not just the warm weather I like. I like it because we see so many of our out-of-state friends in the summer.

JULIE. Speaking of out-of-state friends, I had a visit from a girl I hadn't seen since grade school. She was on her way to Chicago, driving all the way from Denver.

LEON. She must be a pretty good friend, Julie. This is a little out of the way for someone going from Denver to Chicago.

JULIE. Actually, I hardly remembered her.

VAUGHN. She must have remembered you.

JULIE. That's the strange part. She said she remembered how kind I was to her in school when all the other kids were mean to her. I don't remember that at all.

DANNY. Maybe she was thinking of someone else.

JULIE. No, she had a picture of us standing together on the last day of school. I had my arm around her shoulder, and she had this big smile on her face.

ESTELLE. I'll bet you loved Jesus even then.

JULIE. It's true. I loved to pray that God would use me as His helper.

LEON. Well, Julie, maybe the reason you don't even remember being this girl's friend is that you weren't the source of that kindness.

VAUGHN. That story is a great example of what it's like when we turn our lives over to Jesus. His kindness shines through us and on to others, and we aren't even aware of it.

JULIE. To God be the glory.

No Longer Faithless

Hear the word of the LORD, you Israelites, because the LORD has a charge to bring against you who live in the land: "There is no faithfulness, no love, no acknowledgement of God in the land."

Hosea 4:1

Many think of God as the great accuser. In their hearts they know they have done wrong, and they want to have nothing to do with God. They are certain He is waiting for an opportunity to pounce on them with a long list of their transgressions.

And here, in Hosea, we find just such an admonishment. We hear the long-dreaded words, "The Lord has a charge to bring against you who live in the land."

Fearfully, we submit to His anger. "Okay," we say, "Hit me with it." In our minds we start to list our many failures: the times we have lied about others, the goods we have obtained illegally, our immoral behavior. The list is a long and sordid one. We wonder which sins are the ones God will confront us with first.

Well, here's God's list: No faithfulness, no love, no acknowledgment of God.

He is angry because of the way we regard Him. Here we are, afraid to be anywhere in God's vicinity (as though we could be anywhere else; He is omnipresent, you know) for fear of punishment, when we discover that, all along, He has been trying to woo us to His side. He actually wants us to come to Him, to be faithful to Him, to love and to acknowledge Him.

When we refuse to answer the call of a loving God, we live frantic lives. We try to fill our empty hearts with selfish sins. "There is only cursing, lying and murder, stealing and adultery" (Hosea 4:2). "They exchanged their Glory for something disgraceful" (Hosea 4:7).

God's grievance with the Children of Israel, and with us, is explained further in Hosea 4:16: "The Israelites are stubborn, like a stubborn heifer. How then can the Lord pasture them like lambs in a meadow?"

If we would stop running, for a change, we would discover that God is not after us to punish, but to save. He does not want to bring our sins against us, but to take them away. While God hates sin, He loves the sinner.

We need to come to Him in repentance and to let the Holy Spirit work faith in our hearts. Our Heavenly Father will welcome us with open arms. Then, as Jesus lives in our hearts, we will find ourselves faithful, loving, and eager to acknowledge God.

No longer faithless, but faithful to God. Not a God of anger, but a God of love.

Dear Heavenly Father, You are a holy God, and we are not a holy people. Just as the Children of Israel were afraid to come close to the mountain when they sensed Your presence, so too are we often afraid to come near You because of our sin. Forgive us for trying to run from You, and help us to confess our sin, knowing that You are a merciful God. We want to be faithful. We want to let Your love shine through us on to others. Thank you for pursuing us and for showing us love and forgiveness through Jesus Christ our Lord. Amen.

Taking Charge of Your Child's Education

LEON. Boy, did we have fun on our vacation this summer. We must have put two thousand miles on our car. We live in one beautiful country.

VAUGHN. Our family did a lot of camping. We mostly stayed in the area, but you don't have to go far to see beauty in this part of the country.

JULIE. We didn't get away at all. We did have a lot of company, though, and that's just as much fun.

ESTELLE. Our greatest event was the big family reunion on my mother's side. More than 150 folks were there. I got to see gobs of cousins and their kids, and now my nieces and nephews are bringing their kids as well.

JULIE. I envy you, Estelle. Neither my father nor my mother had close-knit families like yours. I think distance just did them in.

LEON. That reunion must have been pure joy.

ESTELLE. Well, not *pure* joy. It was actually sad to see how few of the families are still strong Christians. I mean, most of them go to church now and then, but that's about it.

LEON. I'm sorry to say that is a common occurrence in many of our nation's families today.

ESTELLE. It's very sad for me. We all had very faithful grandparents and parents. My father and his brothers and sisters all had strong ties to the church and strong Christian faiths throughout their lives.

JULIE. Life is hard. Everyone's faith is tested by a lot of ups and downs.

ESTELLE. More ups than downs in our case. Our family has been very blessed. All my cousins have all done well, in a worldly sense. We have doctors, lawyers, even a Navy admiral in our group—strong on worldly achievement but weak on faith.

VAUGHN. I think when things are going well we are quick to take the credit. We think we succeed by our own strength.

ESTELLE. And meanwhile the enemy is there, watching us fail in the only arena that really matters.

LEON. Jesus said, "Be thou faithful unto death and I will give you a crown of life."

JULIE. And being faithful means relying on God's strength, not our own.

Taking Charge of Your Child's Education

Train a child in the way he should go, and when he is old he will not turn from it.

Proverbs 22:6

All of our children went to parochial school. The last thing they did each morning before rushing out the door was to recite to me their memory work for the day, either a Bible passage or a hymn verse or a part of *Luther's Small Catechism*. I am eternally grateful to have had a school that assisted me in teaching my children to know the way they should go.

Education is important, but as parents we need to be closely involved in what it is that our children are learning. I have a friend who is an attorney by profession and the first college graduate in his family. His daughters are bright and went to area schools that their father researched well to be sure they had the classes his daughters would need to get into the colleges of their choice. All three girls have excelled in those colleges and are well on their way to doing great things in their chosen fields.

I had an interesting conversation with my friend the other day. He said that he wished now that he had paid closer attention to what else they were learning. He doesn't know where they got the attitude that homosexuality is simply a different lifestyle. His daughters are uncomfortable when he shares his faith with others. "Dad, everyone has a right to their own beliefs," they tell him. Many of his girls' friends live with their boyfriends outside of marriage, and they do not like him to question the practice. "You shouldn't judge others, Dad," they admonish.

They are lovely girls. It's just that the world does not think like we Christians do. Thus when we leave the education of our children in the hands of the world, the training can go astray.

Stay alert! Watch out for your great enemy, the devil. He prowls around like a roaring lion, looking for someone to devour.

1 Peter 5:8 (NLT)

The devil is looking for a way to devour us and our kids. Admittedly, not every child has the blessing of attending a parochial school. Not every mom is equipped to home school. (I certainly was not.) So what is a parent to do?

Here are a few suggestions:

+ Have regular family devotions. Here is your chance at education. *You* teach your children what it means to be a Christian.

- Talk to your children about the differences that we have with certain viewpoints, i.e., creation versus evolution, life versus choice, etc.

- Memorize Scripture together as a family.

- Pray for your children that they will be unaffected by the world's view of life.

- Be regular in your church and church school attendance. Sunday schools and Bible classes are the church's arm of education. You need all the help you can get.

- Trust God's promise that if you do your part, His word will work in your child's heart. Jesus says, "I have overcome the world."

So make sure you consider "the one thing needful," and don't leave that part up to someone else. You do it. Identify your helpers, beware of the enemy, and entrust your children to Jesus, the one the disciples called, "Teacher."

Almighty Father, we thank You for children. Keep us ever-mindful of our responsibility to bring them up in the nurture and admonition of the Lord. Forgive us for the times we have made the things of this world seem more important in our children's eyes than things of eternal value. Thank you for the educational programs of our churches, for Christian schools, for Christian books and videos, and for all things that help us to raise Christian children. Make us faithful in bringing our children to Jesus so that they may be Your own and live under You in Your kingdom, happy and secure in Your love for them. We pray all this in Jesus' name. Amen.

No Favoritism

VAUGHN. My brother, Jim, is so irritating. He never seems to do anything wrong. The teachers at school were always saying, "Why can't you be more like your brother?"

LEON. What brought that on?

VAUGHN. My parents celebrated their anniversary last week, and Jim bought, "Just the vase I wanted," for Mom, and Dad loved his new fishing rod. Dear old Jim seems to do no wrong.

JULIE. I have a sister like that. Little Miss Perfect. Mom always loved her best.

LEON. That's one thing God does not do. He does not show favoritism.

VAUGHN. Well, didn't He call the Children of Israel to be His "chosen" people?

ESTELLE. He chose them all right. They were going to be His people whether they wanted to or not. And most of the time they didn't want to.

LEON. He chose them for a special purpose, but He did not love them more because of it. God shows no favoritism.

ESTELLE. Sometimes my children accuse me of loving one more than another, and maybe I do treat them differently on different days, but I love them all. I can't imagine having to choose which one is more precious.

JULIE. I really feel sorry for that Australian woman who had to let one of her children go in order to save the other when that tsunami hit them so unexpectedly. She knew she could not save them both.

LEON. Well, thankfully, God never lets any of us go. None is more important than the other. He died for all.

VAUGHN. A beloved brother in Christ. That's how I'm going to think of my brother, Jim, from now on. We are beloved brothers, equally loved by God.

JULIE. Because God shows no favoritism.

No Favoritism

Then Peter began to speak: "I now realize how true it is that God does not show favoritism but accepts men from every nation who fear him and do what is right. You know the message God sent to the people of Israel, telling the good news of peace through Jesus Christ, who is LORD of all."

Acts 10:34–36

Peter had just arrived in Caesarea at the home of Cornelius. It was no small thing for a Jew to enter the home of a gentile, and Cornelius was certainly that. He was a centurion of an Italian Regiment. That means a hundred soldiers were under his command, and he was part of the Roman Empire that was currently ruling over the Jews. Peter was told in a dream to go to Cornelius, and Cornelius, in the verses immediately preceding the verses above, had informed Peter that he, too, had received a message directly from God. An angel had told him to invite Peter to his home.

That is when Peter had an "Aha" experience. "I now realize," he says of his discovery of a great truth, "that God does not show favoritism" (Acts 10:34). As Christians we have been taught that God so loved the world that He sent His Son to redeem the whole world. It is easy to believe that

133

when we lump all peoples into the phrase, "the world." But when we start thinking of individuals that we know, and others that we do not wish to know, it gets harder.

Peter had been told all His life that he was a member of a chosen nation, one picked out of all the peoples of the earth to be set aside as a special race; a nation chosen by God to carry out His plan of redemption, for from this nation would come One who would be a blessing to all the nations. The Children of Israel often forgot that part and just gloried in the fact that they were God's special people. No wonder Peter was amazed at this new understanding about God's love for all people.

We often suffer the same delusion. Most of us admit we are forgiven sinners, but we don't want to be considered sinners on the same level as, well, "real sinners," i.e., thieves, liars, haters, wife beaters, gang members, sexual predators, and murderers. We know that God does love them and He does want them to be saved, but that He loves them as much as He loves us, that He would give His Son to die for one of them if they were the only person on earth, well, that's a little much.

What we have conveniently forgotten is that we need to confess with St. Paul, "I know that nothing good lives in me, that is in my sinful nature" (Romans 7:18). Apart from God, I am no better than any other sinner on this earth. My true nature is totally corrupt. But, through Christ, that changes. I am made clean, just as the repentant liar or thief or murderer is made clean.

God shows no favoritism. He loves us all the same, and He loves us the same all the time. And that is good news for the times we really see our sinful selves. He loves us when we are "good" and when we are "bad," because, when we accept God's forgiveness through Jesus Christ, the "good" comes from His hand and the "bad" is removed as far as the east is from the west.

Some people had parents who withdrew their love when their children displeased them. Well, God is not like that. When we accept Jesus as our Savior and come to God in prayer, He is never distant. God never withdraws His love. And He never loves the "good" Christians more than the "sinful" Christians. He doesn't even love us more when we try to please Him.

He could not love us any more than He already does.

I am Jesus' little lamb
Ever glad at heart I am.
For my shepherd gently guides me,
Knows my needs and well provides me,
Loves me every day the same,
Even calls me by my name.

Henrietta L. von Hayn (1724–1782)

But Now My Eyes Have Seen You

JULIE. Guess what, everybody? I started back to school.

DANNY. I thought one of the biggest reasons to grow up is so that you don't have to go to school.

VAUGHN. That's a brave move, Julie. Are you excited?

JULIE. Mostly, I'm nervous. What if I can't handle the assignments? And I've always been terrified of tests. I'm not used to someone giving me a grade on how well I do something.

DANNY. I get graded on everything—including behavior! That's why I think it will be great to be an adult and have people quit measuring everything I do.

LEON. You don't ever get away from that, Danny. Your boss is going to give evaluations on your job, you'll have to pass a test to get your driver's license, and just wait until you want to buy a house. I can guarantee you'll be judged by your credit rating.

JULIE. I never thought of that, Leon. I guess people have been giving me grades all along, so having a class grade is nothing to be afraid of.

ESTELLE. They even graded Jesus. In our lesson today, they said, "He does all things well."

VAUGHN. If you were arrogant enough to give God a grade I would think you would give Him straight A's for everything.

LEON. Still, don't we sometimes give God bad grades? When something happens that we don't like or don't understand, don't we accuse God of failing? We ask, "Where was God in all of this?"

DANNY. You're right, Leon. I've heard people say, "If there is a God and He is a good God, why did He let such and such happen?"

JULIE. I admit, I've asked that question myself. I guess I've actually tried to decide how well God has performed in my life.

ESTELLE. But when we understand God's love for us in Jesus and all He has done for our salvation, we don't try to evaluate His performance with our limited view. We just say in faith, "He does all things well."

VAUGHN. That's right, Estelle. Faith says, "Straight A's for everything," even when we don't understand.

LEON. Especially when we don't understand.

But Now My Eyes Have Seen You

You said, "Listen now, and I will speak; I will question you, and you shall answer me." My ears had heard of you but now my eyes have seen you. Therefore I despise myself and repent in dust and ashes.

Job 42:4–6

Those of you familiar with the story of Job know that God allowed Satan to bring great trials on his servant, Job. Satan's contention was that it was easy for Job to love God and serve Him as long as life was good. But, if God would allow a little trouble into Job's life, things might change. Satan's challenge? "Let me make his life a little harder and then see if he remains faithful."

As Job falls victim to all sorts of calamities, his friends come to give him insight into why he deserves to be punished. Job defends himself, saying he has done nothing to provoke God's wrath. This goes on for a while, and then God steps in to ask Job some pretty potent questions:

Will the one who contends with the Almighty correct Him? Would you discredit my justice? Would you condemn me to justify yourself? Do you have an arm like God's and can your voice thunder like his?

Job 40:2, 8–9

Have you ever questioned God's plan for your life? Are you upset with God because things have not turned out the way you had envisioned? Are you currently going through a hardship that you do not think you deserve? Are you a little bit (or a lot) angry with God?

Welcome to Job's world. As we read though this story, we see Job going through all these feelings. He never got to the place of cursing God, but he was not happy with events. "Where is God when it counts?" he must have asked. "If only I could lay my case before Him, he would see the unfairness of it all."

Job says, "My ears had heard of you." He thought he knew all about God and his gracious mercy. We, too, have some well-formed ideas about God. We have an agenda for Him, as concerns our lives. We even think we know how He thinks. Have you ever heard anyone make the statement, "How could a loving God allow such a thing to happen?"

The surprising part of the story is that when Job gets his chance to bring his case before God, we see a different response than the one we would expect. "My ears had heard of you, but now my eyes have seen you. Therefore I despise myself and repent in dust and ashes" (Job 42:5).

When facing the true God, not the invention of his own heart, Job is humbled. His first thought is to repent. He humbly asks forgiveness for the arrogance of his reasoning, for daring to think he deserved anything but God's wrath.

And that needs to be our position, as well. God is gracious to us sinners, even to the point of sending His Son to die for our sins, but He owes us nothing. We indeed deserve nothing from His hand but wrath. That's why God's goodness toward us is called grace: *undeserved* love.

The story ends with God blessing Job with family and riches far beyond what he lost. But, if you were to ask Job, the best part of the story was that he received those gifts from God in true humility, knowing that none of it was of his own doing. He learned that God gives freely to those who have no claim on Him.

And that is good news for us.

Gracious Father, many times we rebel against Your plans for our lives. When bad things happen to us, we even accuse You of being unfair. Like Job, we want to defend ourselves. We confess that we have not always seen You as You really are, that we have created our own version of You within our sinful hearts. Remember, we are only dust. Forgive our arrogance, and let us see You in all Your glory, so that we, like Job, may realize our utter worthlessness and acknowledge the greatness of Your grace toward us. Thank You for sending Jesus to save us from the death and punishment that we deserve. In His name we pray. Amen.

Rooted and Built Up

LEON. How is everyone this week?

JULIE. I have had a rotten week. Everything that could go wrong did, and even those things that went okay took three times as long to accomplish.

DANNY. School starts next week. That just about sums it up for me.

VAUGHN. Take a look at my bank balance, and that will tell you how my life is going.

LEON. I'm sorry I asked.

VAUGHN. Sometimes I feel like God is far away. Where is He when the real problems hit?

ESTELLE. You guys remind me of the old farm couple driving along in the truck. The wife looked over at her husband, who was driving, and said, "Remember when we used to snuggle up whenever we went somewhere in the truck? It seemed like we couldn't get close enough when we'd drive around. You wanted to be right next to me all the time."

JULIE. I remember those times.

ESTELLE. Well, the farmer took one look at his wife, then looked back at the road, and drawled, "Well, I ain't moved."

LEON. That's good, Estelle. When we whine to God that He is not close enough, He just answers, "I ain't moved."

VAUGHN. You know, now that I think about it, last year we were much more faithful with family devotions, and I felt a lot closer to God. I don't remember being so concerned about money last year.

JULIE. What's that saying you always bring up, Estelle? "Look at the world and be distressed. Look at yourself and be depressed—"

DANNY. "Look at Christ and be at rest."

Rooted and Built Up

So then, just as you received Christ Jesus as LORD, continue to live in him, rooted and built up in him, strengthened in the faith as you were taught, and overflowing with thankfulness.

Colossians 2:6

Can you remember the last time you were overflowing with thankfulness for your salvation in Jesus Christ? This verse in Colossians directs us to remember our response when we first came to faith. "So, then, just as you received Christ Jesus as Lord."

I do not remember a time when I did not belong to the family of God. I had godly parents and was taught the scriptures from childhood, just like Saint Timothy who was taught to love God at his mother's and grandmother's knees as Paul tells us in 2 Timothy 1:5. I do recall having a wonderfully secure childhood, and I remember having a thankful heart.

Paradoxically, when we "continue to live in him, rooted and built up in him, strengthened in the faith we were taught," as St. Paul continues in Colossians 2:6, we do not become more independent in our thinking, but more child-like, more like when we first came to faith. The more we mature as Christians, the less we move in our own strength.

The more we know about God, the less we worry about ourselves. We do not need, nor do we desire, to stand on our own. We become eager to rely on God's will for our lives.

The ideology of rugged individualism, embraced by many Americans, becomes distasteful. We don't stand on our own beliefs; we stand on the promises of God. We don't worry about God's disapproval of our lives of sin; we bask in His wonderful forgiveness. We move through our days with the joy and security of well-loved children. Attached to the vine that is Christ, we let His goodness flow into good works that please Him.

That is the freedom of the Gospel. That is why, as rooted Christians, we are built up in our Lord and are strengthened by a faith that overflows with thanksgiving, grateful for a life of quiet joy. Our lives may not be free from the troubles of this world, but they are free from the anxiety and anguish those troubles would otherwise bring. And we find ourselves just as blissful as when we first believed.

Chief of sinners though I be,
Jesus lived and died for me.
Died that I might live on high,
Lived that I might never die.
As the branch is to the vine,
I am His and He is mine.
Chief of sinners though I be,
Christ is All in all to me;

All my wants to Him are known,
All my sorrows are His own.
He sustains the hidden life
Safe with Him from earthly strife.

William McComb (1793–1873)

Doing it God's Way

LEON. Welcome back from summer, everybody. I hope your summer has been as interesting as mine has been. I went for two weeks to one of those elder hostels on a college campus. I took a course on astronomy and one on cake decorating.

LISA. Boy, I envy you for the one on cake decorating. My mother used to bake cakes for weddings, and I loved to watch her work.

VAUGHN. I've had a great time. I went backpacking and kayaking in the mountains of Georgia. That is beautiful country.

ESTELLE. We went to a family reunion in Georgia. You're right, Vaughn, that is spectacular country. Our get-together was way back in "them thar hills."

LISA. That sounds wonderful. I've never been to Georgia.

ALAN. My brothers and I went on the best fishing trip ever. We were at a lake in Northern Canada that was huge. We rarely saw another boat, and the weather was beautiful every day we were there.

LISA. I love to fish.

LEON. Where did you go this summer, Lisa?

LISA. Well, I guess I pretty much just went between my house and my sister's house. She lives four blocks from me.

VAUGHN. That doesn't sound too adventurous. Wouldn't you like to see more of the world than that?

LISA. I'd love to travel, but, well, my sister was diagnosed with multiple sclerosis several years ago, and now she has real trouble getting around. I try to make sure the rest of my family gets in a vacation or two, but I stay pretty close to home. She can't do much for herself anymore.

ALAN. It's too bad about your sister, Lisa. I feel like you are missing out on a lot of things.

LISA. Not at all. I have had a wonderful summer. I love my sister and I don't feel put out in the least bit. It is a great privilege to be of help. I'm sure the time for travel will come someday.

ESTELLE. Actually, Alan, I think maybe we are the ones missing out. Here we are, running around having a good time for ourselves, and here is Lisa, quietly living like Jesus, having compassion on others, and feeling the peace and joy that always comes when we are doing God's will.

Doing it God's Way

As Jesus was getting into the boat, the man who had been demon-possessed begged to go with him. Jesus did not let him, but said, "Go home to your family and tell them how much the LORD has done for you, and how he has had mercy on you."

Mark 5:18–19

Jesus had just healed a man who had been demon-possessed. The man's gratitude knew no bounds. Eager to follow Jesus to the ends of the earth, willing to drop everything and go wherever Jesus led, he wanted to tell everyone about God's love.

That is a picture of devotion many of us yearn to have for our Lord and Savior. We long to say, "Here am I, send me, send me." We want to be willing to head off to deepest Africa or to China or to the cold northern provinces of Canada with the sole purpose of spreading the love of Jesus Christ to the nations of the world.

Some of us have held this vision of mission work since childhood. And yet many of us find ourselves in our same little world. Most of us haven't even gone as far as the neighboring town to share our faith.

Well, take heart. When the man healed of demon-possession offers to follow Jesus, the Bible passage says, "Jesus did not let him." That is not the response we might have expected, but God's ways are higher than our ways. Jesus had a plan for this man's life. He recognized the man's desire to serve. He did not reject the offer; He just changed the assignment.

"Go home to your family and tell them how much the Lord has done for you, and how he has shown mercy on you." That, Jesus tells the man, is how he can best serve God's plan. It was not at all what the man had envisioned.

Sometimes God's assignment can surprise and dismay us, as well. A young mother, following the daily monotony of household chores and the demanding task of caring for small children, may feel as though her opportunity to serve is non-existent. A faithful church member, caught in a dead-end job, trying to make a living for his family, might long for a chance to spread the Gospel to those in a faraway land. A child who wants to tell everyone about Jesus doesn't know how to make a difference. And, to all of them, Jesus says, "Go home to your family and tell them how much the Lord has done for you."

Maybe you are not in the full-time ministry or in some foreign mission field, because you are like the man in our story. He wanted to follow his Lord to a far-off place, but, the Bible says, "Jesus did not let him." Have you ever stopped to consider that Jesus might already have you in the exact place He wants you to serve?

My father used to say, "If you, who love your children with all your heart, fail to bring them the good news of salvation, who do you think is going to love them enough to do it for you?" And that means speaking about God's goodness to cousins and friends, to parents and brothers and sisters and aunts and uncles, all those people who live in that place we call home. If we, who love them, do not tell them, who do you think will do it for us?

My favorite part of this story is the next verse: "So the man went away and began to tell in the Decapolis how much Jesus had done for him. And all the people were amazed" (Mark 5:20). He went back home, but he brought with him a willing heart and a message of good news, and he "wowed" them, right there in his own backyard.

So, we need to stay home, if that is our assignment at the moment, and let God use us to amaze even folks who have known us all our lives. With God's power we will make a difference for the people that we care about most—mission work at its finest, because it is God's plan.

Dear Father in Heaven, teach us to simply be available, willing to go where you send us, even if you call us to stay right where we are at this moment. Let our hearts be full of the wonder of all you do for us, and let that wonder spill over to our family and friends. Open our mouths to speak of the kindness You have shown through the death of Your Son, Jesus Christ, that our family and friends may know You and Your great love for them. We pray this in Jesus' holy name. Amen.

Eternal Things

ESTELLE. Are you going to the women's retreat next weekend, Dixie?

DIXIE. I'd like to, but I just hate to leave my dog at home overnight.

LEON. Don't you have a neighbor or something that could let the dog out a couple of times while you are gone?

DIXIE. Oh, sure. I could take care of her physical needs pretty easily; it's her emotional needs that I worry about.

VAUGHN. Dogs have emotional needs that we humans are to care for?

DIXIE. Oh, yeah. I know my dog gets real lonely if I'm gone too much. As long as I have owned her, I haven't left her alone for even one night. (Says proudly.)

LEON. Well, if you aren't going to the retreat, our evangelism group is going to go around the neighborhood on Saturday morning and hang a little bag of information on doors. We need all the folks we can get. Can you help us out?

DIXIE. I work full time, you know, and Saturday is the one day I try to set aside to take my dog on an outing. There is this new park we want to check out.

VAUGHN. If that's the park over on Robert Street, it's pretty nice. Our church helped put up some of the new play equipment last month. By the way, if anyone can help out, they are still accepting donations. That playground stuff is more expensive than we thought.

DIXIE. I was going to give to that fund. I even had money set aside for it. But then my dog had to have emergency surgery, and I had to use it for that. I was glad I had a little extra cash around. You would never believe how much that set me back!

ESTELLE. I'm a little uncomfortable saying this, Dixie, but I've noticed that our society has turned a lot of time and energy to the care of pets and other animals, sometimes to the neglect of care for other people.

DIXIE. Well, people can be pretty unpleasant, but my dog is always happy to see me.

VAUGHN. That may be true, but we must never lose sight of our real task here on earth.

LEON. Love the Lord your God with all your heart, with all your soul and with all your mind, and, love your neighbor as yourself. That is the whole summary of God's law.

ESTELLE. Animals are a part of God's creation. Sure, we care for the creation, but God wants us to be about His business, the business of saving the lost and dying.

DIXIE. I see what you are saying. I never thought of it that way before. It's okay to love my dog, but it's not okay if I let that interfere with spending time on eternal things.

VAUGHN. God should always come first in our lives.

Eternal Things

Lift up your eyes to the heavens, look at the earth beneath; the heavens will vanish like smoke, the earth will wear out like a garment and its inhabitants die like flies. But my salvation will last forever, my righteousness will never fail.

Isaiah 51:6

One of the popular themes of our day is man's attempt to preserve the environment. As Christians, we too like to be good stewards of God's creation. But did you ever stop to think that there is danger in this pursuit?

God tells us, through these words of Isaiah, to take a good look around us. He wants us to see the heavens in all their majesty and to look at the wonders of the earth below and to know this: Someday these things will vanish. They are a gift of the Creator. They do not belong to us. There is no "Mother Earth."

We are actually being warned in this verse about making something that is temporary our life's main focus. "My salvation will last forever; my righteousness will never fail." God wants us to be about the business of eternal things—to serve the Creator, not His creation.

Satan is the ruler of this world. He would gladly direct our attention to things that do not last. The unhealthy preoccupation with animals is one way in which we are straying from loving the Giver of Life. "Do you love your cat or dog more than me?" might be Jesus' question to our day. Or "Do you spend more money and time in a year on your cat or dog (or the Humane Society or the Sierra Club) than you spend giving toward and doing God's work of bringing His salvation to the lost and dying?"

We don't like these questions. "I think everyone should be kind to animals," we counter. "Isn't it part of our work to care for the land?" we lament.

To be kind to animals, yes. To take care of the land, yes. To care for (love) them? Maybe not. God calls us to love *Him* with *all* our heart, with *all* our soul, and with *all* our mind.

We who seek to love God must subject the creation, and all that is in it, to Him. Not a popular thought, but one that is necessary to separate the world's teaching from God's own. The Bible does not speak about loving animals. Did you know that? God has not instructed us to save the environment. He knows it cannot be saved. It was doomed when man sinned, and one day it will "wear out like a garment." Who are we to attempt to prove God wrong?

Jesus once said to a man who sought to follow him but wanted to tend to the things of this world first, "Follow me, and let the dead bury their own dead" (Matthew 8: 22).

Perhaps He is, in essence, saying to His followers, "Let those who are dead in their sins take on the hopeless task of saving the earth. You know it is dying and will indeed some-day pass away. You be about those things that last into eternity—the Word of God and people."

Many will find this an unpopular view to take, but the verse following says, "Hear me you who know what is right, you people who have my law in your hearts: Do not fear the reproach of men or be terrified of their insults. For the moth will eat them up like a garment; the worm will devour them like wool. But my righteousness will last forever, my salvation through all generations" (Isaiah 51:7–8).

Almighty Father, teach us the right way to regard Your creation. Fix our eyes on Jesus and not on the things of this world, even though they are good things, gifts from Your gracious hand. May we be good stewards of the land and kind to animals, but deliver us from the sin of making them more important than You intend them to be. Keep us ever-mindful of the new heavens and the new earth and our citizenship in that world. We look to You for direction in all we do and say. We ask these things in the name of the Eternal Son of Righteousness, Jesus Christ, our Lord. Amen.

The Lord's

VAUGHN. I'm trying to think of a good way to show a friend of mine how much I care about her.

JULIE. They have some really nice greeting cards at the drug store.

VAUGHN. I was thinking of a bigger gesture.

LEON. You could rent a billboard or get a pilot to pull one of those big signs behind a plane.

JULIE. Or you could take her to a ballgame and have something put up on the electronic board.

VAUGHN. Maybe something more personal than that. Not something the whole world would see.

ESTELLE. How about getting a tattoo?

All look at Estelle with surprise.

VAUGHN. A tattoo?

ESTELLE. My great-grandmother had a tattoo.

They all look at Estelle again.

JULIE. What did it say?

ESTELLE. She wouldn't tell me.

LEON. Where was it?

ESTELLE. Great-Grandpa wouldn't tell me.

JULIE. Somehow that is too little information and more information than I wanted to know all at the same time.

VAUGHN. I think I'll just send flowers. But thanks for the suggestions.

The Lord's

One will say, "I belong to the LORD"; another will call himself by the name of Jacob; still another will write on his hand, "The LORD's."

Isaiah 44:5

"Still another will write on his hand, 'The Lord's.'" Can you picture that? A tattoo in the Bible? Someone writing on his hand? Why would he do that?

First and foremost, the writer wants to show that he no longer considers himself a free man, nor does he hide that fact. It is written on his person for all to see: "The Lord's," he writes. Furthermore, this "brand," as it were, is not placed there by someone else. It is the writer himself who engraves the words onto his own hand.

Does he do this of his own initiative? I don't think so. In Isaiah 44:1, God speaks to Israel, "Whom I have chosen." God chose Israel, and He chooses us, "While we were yet sinners"; nevertheless, this individual heeds God's call and responds with zeal.

Don't you just long to submit, as did this writer? To proclaim to all that you belong to God? To see that reminder each time your hands are used in His service?

Then everything you do becomes a reflection of your Owner. As you belong to Him, so does all that you possess belong to Him. Not your talent, His. Not your thoughts, His. You become the servant, carrying out the will of the Master.

Today, I boldly engraved a tattoo of my own. Right there on my hand, I wrote, "The Lord's," both physically and metaphorically. How simple. What a wonderful way to bring all these things to mind!

Get out your pens, you called of God. Go ahead. Write it. You will never do anything more profound!

Take my life, and let it be consecrated, Lord, to Thee.
Take my moments and my days; let them flow in ceaseless praise.

Take my hands, and let them move at the impulse of Thy love.
Take my feet, and let them be swift and beautiful for Thee.

Take my voice, and let me sing always, only, for my King.
Take my lips, and let them be filled with messages from Thee.

Take my silver and my gold; not a mite would I withhold.
Take my intellect, and use every power as Thou shalt choose.

Take my will, and make it Thine; it shall be no longer mine.
Take my heart, it is Thine own; it shall be Thy royal throne.

Take my love, my Lord, I pour at Thy feet its treasure store.
Take myself, and I will be ever, only, all for Thee.

Francis Havergal (1874)

God's Perfect Law

ESTELLE. I've had an interesting week.

LEON. Why, did you win a trip to Hawaii?

DANNY. Did you fall off a ladder?

VAUGHN. Did you buy a chicken farm?

ESTELLE. None of the above.

JULIE. So, what made your week interesting?

ESTELLE. I had a huge fight with my neighbor. She gets really angry because the pine cones from our evergreen always blow into her yard and onto her roof, clogging her gutters.

LEON. What does she want you to do about it? Cut down the tree?

ESTELLE. Exactly. But it's the only big tree in our yard, and we have no interest in cutting it down.

VAUGHN. That's a pretty drastic request. I mean, stuff like that can't be helped. Did you tell her off?

ESTELLE. No, I baked her a pie.

JULIE. You baked her a pie?

DANNY. And threw it in her face, right?

ESTELLE. Of course not.

VAUGHN. You baked the pie to try to appease her, right?

ESTELLE. No, I baked her a pie because I read one time that when you were angry with someone, the best thing for you to do is to do something loving toward them.

JULIE. I don't think I would feel like baking her a pie.

ESTELLE. I didn't say I felt like doing it; I just did it. I just asked God to show love to her through me, even though I did not feel loving toward her. And it worked.

VAUGHN. What do you mean? Did she apologize for the tree thing?

ESTELLE. No. She told me if I thought that a silly old pie was going to clean out her gutters, I had another think coming.

LEON. So, how can you say this pie thing worked?

ESTELLE. It didn't change *her* attitude toward *me*, but by following God's command to love my neighbor and by using *His* power, I found that *I* was no longer angry with *her*. I was able to love her.

JULIE. God's love is a powerful thing, and obeying God's commands keeps us free of the separating effect of sin.

God's Perfect Law

But the man who looks intently into the perfect law that gives freedom, and continues to do this, not forgetting what he has heard, but doing it—he will be blessed in what he does.

James 1:25

There were several James' mentioned in the New Testament. Two of Jesus' disciples were named James: James the brother of John and James the son of Alphaeus. But the author of the book of James has been commonly understood to be James, the brother of Jesus, the overseer of the Judean Church. He was highly regarded and was known as a warrior of prayer. His countrymen called him "James the Just."

It is this James who tells us that God's perfect law gives freedom. Many people rebel at the imposition of the law. They see laws as restricting their freedom, not obtaining it. But "James the Just" tells us to look to God's laws for true freedom.

How can laws create freedom? Well, the child with a fenced backyard has freedom of movement the parents would not allow without the presence of the fence, and we, too, have God-given parameters within which we find this same kind of freedom. It is a freedom from harm, as it were.

To find those parameters, we must look intently into God's Word to discover what He says. We need to be familiar with biblical teachings. And it doesn't stop there. We have to keep at it; we have to develop a lifelong practice of seeking to know God's will as revealed through His Word.

And then the main part; with God's help, we have to do it. Often when I would caution my children to be careful or remind them of a household rule or deadline, they would answer impatiently, "I know." But, as I regularly informed them, knowing and doing are two different things.

That's what James is reminding us in this book. Later in this letter he also points out, "Anyone, then, who knows the good he ought to do and doesn't do it, sins" (James 4:17). Knowing and doing are two different things.

The real message of these verses, however, is that when we see God's law as something freeing, and when we do follow God's directives, our efforts are blessed. The husband and wife who remain faithful to their wedding vows, the children who respect and obey their parents, and the family that worships together faithfully, all experience the blessings that flow from obedience.

Did you recognize that those were examples of obeying three of the Ten Commandments: Do not commit adultery, honor your father and mother, and remember the Sabbath Day to keep it holy? Freeing laws that, when studied and followed, result in lives blessed by the Father who knows what is best for us and in lives filled with God's forgiveness for the times we fail.

May we your precepts, Lord, fulfill
And do on earth our Father's will
As angels do above;
Still walk in Christ, the living way,
With all your children and obey
The law of Christian love.

Edward Osler (1798–1863)

Happy Lives

LEON. Well, I really had a good week.

VAUGHN. What happened?

LEON. Absolutely nothing. That's why it was a good week.

JULIE. Things have been crazy around our house. My mom is in the hospital, my daughter is having a lot of trouble with one of her new teachers at school, and now we found out that my husband is facing a huge reorganization at work.

ESTELLE. I remember times like that. I hated the uncertainty. There was so much to worry about. What if this, and what if that?

JULIE. I'm ashamed to admit it, but I woke up last night with a panic attack. I was so overwhelmed I could hardly catch my breath. It was a scary feeling.

VAUGHN. Oh, you get those, too?

JULIE. The best part was that I had somewhere to go. I went to God in prayer. It wasn't long before I settled down. Once I realized that I was not in charge and handed my problems back to God, I felt peaceful again. I actually slept like a baby after that.

LEON. What do people do when they have a week like yours and don't know God's loving hand in their life?

ESTELLE. I hadn't really thought about it. Maybe I should be more aware of how desperate people are for real answers. I know my friend Carla is having a tough time right now. I don't think she has any connection with a church or anything. I should give her a call.

VAUGHN. I think if I had a panic attack and didn't have God to turn to, I'd, well, *panic*.

LEON. Thanks be to God that we do not live lives of desperation, wondering how things will turn out. We can claim His promise that all things will work for good for those who love Him and are living according to His purpose.

ESTELLE. We can actually be happy.

Happy Lives

Happy is the man who is always reverent, but he who hardens his heart will fall into calamity.

Proverbs 28:14 (NKJV)

I usually use the New International Version of the Bible, but for this verse I liked the New King James Version because of the use of the word "happy." The word "blessed," used by the NIV, seems less clear to me, perhaps because we often relate the word "blessings" to material possessions. If we are blessed, we have reason to be happy, yet, happiness does not hinge on having material possessions. Happiness is a blessing in itself. How could those who are always reverent, always conscious of the work of Almighty God in their lives, be anything but happy?

And yet, you and I know unhappy Christians. Why is that? I have been a child of God for as long as I can remember. I had faithful, Christian parents who taught me early about Jesus' love for me, and I clearly remember knowing that Jesus had died for my sins at a very young age. I grew up in a happy home and have had a happy life. My children are grown now and live in happy homes of their own.

Sound like the American dream? Can anyone really make those statements with a clear conscience? Well, according to

King Solomon, who wrote this verse in Proverbs, it is possible, indeed. Happiness is not just something others have; it is something that can be ours as well.

Abraham Lincoln is reported to have said, "I think a man is about as happy as he decides he is going to be." While there is truth to that statement, God says there are certain things that are a precursor to happiness. Reverence is mentioned here, and the absence of reverence, a hardened heart, does not lead to happiness, but calamity.

Have the calamities in your life given a foothold to unhappiness? There is a cure for that. God spells out for Christians the formula for a happy life. His word was written with the desire to give us a deeper understanding of the things that lead to happiness.

This is in no way meant to disparage those who have been sad most of their lives. Chemical imbalance and physiological causes can lead to clinical depressions over which one has little control. Traumatic events, especially ones early in a child's life, can leave scars that can include an underlying sadness.

Nevertheless, Scripture says, "Happy is the man who…" God says we can be happy. How is this achieved? By having a better understanding of what God has revealed about Himself, we know Him better. The more we know of Him, the more we love Him, and the more we stand in awe of the mighty things He has done on our behalf. Knowing leads to reverence, and, "Happy is the man [and woman and child] who is always reverent."

Dear Heavenly Father, You are mighty in all Your works. We praise You for Your promise to care for us, and we give into Your hands all the concerns and disappointments of this life. Forgive us for times of complaining and doubt. Resting in Your love for us through our Lord and Savior, Jesus Christ, we thank You that even in the midst of trials and sadness we know a quiet joy. We dare to be happy because You are our Lord and our Redeemer. In Jesus' name we pray. Amen.

It's Not My Fault

LEON. I am very concerned about my cousin.

JULIE. Is he ill?

LEON. Not in the physical sense, but I think you could say he's sick, if sin is a sickness. He's a con artist.

VAUGHN. There really are people like that? I thought they just made those guys up.

LEON. No, he's for real. He is always coming up with some scam or another.

ESTELLE. And I suppose he is rolling in dough with his ill-gotten gains.

LEON. Not at all; quite the opposite, in fact. Most of his grand schemes either fall through or land him in hot water. He just got out prison after serving a five-year term for investment fraud, and he's already got big ideas for his next shady venture.

JULIE. You'd think he'd learn after a while.

LEON. No kidding. But the worst part is that nothing is ever his fault. He thinks the police are just picking on him or his partners let him down or some smart aleck messed up his ideas.

ESTELLE. I suppose if it is never his fault, he'll never quit doing what he does. He's convinced himself that the next one will be the big one.

LEON. And, if it is never his fault, he'll never seek forgiveness or see the need for a Savior.

JULIE. Satan must be laughing at our stupidity when we fall for his schemes. His cons never make us happy and usually make us fall flat on our faces.

VAUGHN. Well, I have to confess, I'm one of those guys who hates to be wrong. But now you've made me think. I need to be more honest with myself; I need to admit that I sin.

It's Not My Fault

He who is pregnant with evil and conceives trouble
gives birth to disillusionment.

Psalm 7:14

Don't you just love it when the psalmist tells it like it is? King David writes that troublemakers are the begetters of their own disenchantment. They let Satan trick them into thinking they will be happy if they give in to the sinful desires of their hearts, when nothing could be further from the truth.

And nothing could be further from the mind of the sinner than that it is his own fault that things do not go well for him. The man who continually berates and belittles his wife is devastated when she leaves him. "Why doesn't she love me anymore?" he cries out in bewilderment.

"My son is a good boy," laments a brokenhearted mother. "It was not his fault his passengers did not have on their seatbelts. He would never willingly hurt anybody. How can he be tried for manslaughter? What if he promises to never drink and drive again?"

Have you ever heard refrains along these lines?

Not long ago, a retired schoolteacher shared that he could predict what a student would say when asked by a fellow student how he or she had done on a test.

"If the student got an A or a B," the teacher explained, "the answer would be, 'I got an A, or I got a B.' If, however, the grade was a C, D, or F, the answer was always, 'The teacher gave me a C, or D, or F.'"

And along comes David, the psalmist, to spell it out for us in plain words: "He who is pregnant with evil and conceives trouble gives birth to disillusionment." Things do not turn out as Satan claimed they would. Instead, you have fathered your own "bad luck."

The following verse says it quite well, too. "He who digs a hole and scoops it out falls into the pit he has made" (Psalm 7:15).

Parents, quit making excuses for your children, and hold them responsible for their actions. Prideful sinner, you need to own up to your sinful choices, as well. God is merciful to the penitent sinner, but how can he forgive you for something that is always somebody else's fault?

"If we claim to be without sin, we deceive ourselves, and the truth is not in us. If we confess our sins, he is faithful and just and will forgive us our sins and purify us from all unrighteousness" (1 John 1:8, 9).

Loving Father, we confess to You our many sins. It is hard for us to admit wrongdoing. We often believe that our reasons for making certain choices have validity and that those reasons somehow justify our actions. We confess, too, that we hold others to a higher standard than the one to which we hold ourselves and so we are quick to judge and slow to repent. As we come closer to Your holiness, we see how corrupt we are. Reassure us that our sin will not separate us from Your love. Thank You that You love us when we deserve nothing but punishment and death; that while we were yet sinners, Christ died for us. Humble us and forgive us through Your Son, Jesus Christ, our Lord and Savior. Amen.

God's Math

LEON. Well, how's life going for all of you? Are you starting to get into the holiday spirit? Thanksgiving is right around the corner, you know.

JULIE. I don't get it. It's the time of the year we should be most happy and thankful, but it seems that this is the very time things get tense around our house.

VAUGHN. In other words, you and your husband had a big fight, right?

JULIE. Who told you about that?

VAUGHN. Nobody had to tell me. This is fight season, didn't you know?

ESTELLE. Money problems, huh?

JULIE. Who told you that?

LEON. Nobody had to tell us, Julie. We're all married. Anything specific?

JULIE. Not really. The credit card statement came, and my husband blew up and accused me of overspending. I said,

"Wait a minute, Buster. I'm not overspending; you're just under-depositing!"

LEON. It may sound strange, but my wife and I don't fight much about money anymore.

VAUGHN. I suppose you're pretty well positioned by now.

LEON. It's not that. It's just that we've seen God get us through so many hard times that we have no qualms about trusting His provision for us. We've tried to get ahead by limiting our giving at church, and we've tried to give way more than we thought we could afford, and God has been faithful. We never got ahead when we "under" gave, and we never fell behind when we "over" gave.

JULIE. That's interesting. You mean you were able to give generously toward God's kingdom, and your financial situation was unaffected?

LEON. I didn't say it was unaffected. I said we didn't see a change in our bottom line. What changed was our lack of worry about the money situation.

ESTELLE. And so, no fights. I get it. When you trust in God for your family's financial future, you can give freely, still have plenty, be truly thankful, and not let the problem of money dominate your life.

JULIE. I think we need to pray about this at our house. To be able to give generously and have no more fights about money would be something to be really thankful for.

God's Math

But just as you excel in everything—in faith, in speech, in knowledge, in complete earnestness and in your love for us—see that you also excel in this grace of giving.

2 Corinthians 8:7

Whenever my husband and I take a look at our current situation, we just shake our heads and say, "God's math." You see, we live in a very nice town home and drive a nice car. We have no idea how this occurred.

We have been "tithers" ever since the first days of our marriage. It is just something we have always done. We do not really give it much thought. It is a way of life, a habit with us. I don't ever remember thinking that if only we would cut back our offerings, we would have more for ourselves. It just never occurred to us.

We raised eight children in a parsonage on a rural minister's salary. Some years our children's new school supplies consisted of pencils with their names on them that my coupon-conscious husband sent for with carefully collected box tops from cereal boxes, but every year we had an outrageous amount of fun. We lived on one of the best sledding hills in Minnesota, and at least once a winter we would wake the kids up in the middle of the night when the moon was full and take them sledding. We flew kites. We had a parachute (bought at one of my weekly garage sale outings) that, when tied high in a tree, would support at least three kids who floated aloft, cradled at the bottom of its silken shell.

We sang as a family and traveled all over the United States to sing in churches. We were on the road in a converted school bus that meant more to us than any motor home. We had fun.

All our children went to a Christian grade school, a Christian high school, and all have graduated from college, four with master's degrees. Tuition was a way of life.

I don't say this to brag. I say it with the same amazement with which you read it. How could this be? No one can afford a big family anymore. I agree.

It seemed like money was pretty tight at the time, and yet it didn't. I know that I knew where every penny went. (I told my husband that we had turned some kind of miraculous corner the other day. I found twenty-one dollars in the drier that I didn't even know I had lost.) But all I really remember was the wonderful time we had. I remember thinking how privileged I was to live with these wonderful people: my husband and my children.

And now we live in a nice house and drive a nice car. How did that happen? Weren't we sacrificing our all for our Lord and our family? And so we shake our heads and say, "God's math." It just must be "God's math."

We give Thee but Thine own,
Whate'er the gift may be;
All that we have is Thine alone,
A trust, O Lord, from Thee.
May we Thy bounties thus
As stewards true receive,
And gladly, as Thou blessest us,
To Thee our firstfruits give.

William W. How (1864)

Giving Thanks

LEON. I can't believe the Thanksgiving holiday is right around the corner already.

ESTELLE. I hear more complaining than thanksgiving most of the time.

JULIE. There's a ton of grumbling going on at work, that's for sure.

VAUGHN. When I was a kid, it took too much time to grumble at my house.

ESTELLE. That's silly, Vaughn. Why, I can grumble and work at the same time.

VAUGHN. Well, if my mom caught you grumbling, she would make you stop whatever you were doing and write down five things you were grateful for.

LEON. That's a great idea—making us turn our grumbling hearts into thankful ones.

VAUGHN. Well, it's not so great when you're ten years old. I remember one time grumbling to Mom about my brother getting to play ball before his homework was done, but she was making me finish mine. Not only did I have to finish my homework, but now, because I grumbled about it, I had to write a list. Of course, when I complained about that, she made me write five more things to be thankful for.

JULIE. Well, I can easily think of ten things for which I'm thankful.

VAUGHN. Well, I couldn't, and when I complained about that, the list grew to fifteen. I had to add peas and asparagus just to have enough things to get out of there.

LEON. I'll bet she teased you about that.

VAUGHN. Every time we had peas or asparagus.

JULIE. Still, that's a wonderful way to remember all the blessings God gives to us each day.

ESTELLE. Let's do that right now. Let's write down five things for which we're thankful.

LEON. I don't know. I hate making lists. Anyway, I don't have a pen.

JULIE. Now that's ten things for you, Leon.

Giving Thanks

Though the fig tree does not bud and there are no grapes on the vines, though the olive crop fails and the fields produce no food, though there are no sheep in the pen and no cattle in the stalls, yet I will rejoice in the LORD, I will be joyful in God my Savior.

Habakkuk 3:17–18

Remember when you were in school and the teacher had the class write out things for which they were thankful? Many kids wrote, "I'm thankful for my family" and followed that up with a fairly recognizable drawing of their mom and dad, brothers and sisters. Others wrote, "I'm thankful for food" or "I'm thankful for my house."

Some kids made long lists:

- Name of best friend.
- Favorite toy.
- Favorite food.
- Favorite pet.
- Favorite subject in school.

The last one was probably for the benefit of the teacher. But all in all the lists made us realize the many blessings God had sent our way.

I remember a poem in which one line read, "Thank You for the birds that sing; thank You, God, for everything." That summed things up nicely in my mind. All blessings come from God, so why not thank Him all at once? "Thank You, God, for everything."

Well, the prophet Habakkuk gives a different list than the ones of bounty that I remember from my classmates. His list?

- No buds on the fig tree.
- No grapes on the vines.
- No olive crops this year.
- No produce from the fields.
- No sheep in the pen.
- No cattle in the stalls.

Oh, and thank You, God, for everything.

Some of you are not harboring a spirit of gratitude. You have had a financial setback. You have recently lost a loved one. You are lonely. You are sick. *All* your favorite candidates lost in the last election. You think you have nothing for which to be thankful.

The prophet Habakkuk shows us that true thankfulness is tied to one thing, and one thing only: our relationship to God. And when that relationship is in place, gratitude becomes a way of life. It is no longer dependent on our circumstances.

God loves us with His whole heart, far beyond what we could know or imagine. If we could grasp that truth, we would accept from His hand both the "good" and the "bad" with indifference, hence Habakkuk's list.

Martin Luther made a similar confession of faith in the great Reformation hymn, *A Mighty Fortress is Our God*. He says, "And take they our:

- life
- goods
- fame
- child or
- wife

Let these all be gone. They yet have nothing won. The kingdom's ours forever."

So, make your thanksgiving list. And, remember to put it all down, both the "good" and the "bad." And then, because of God's love for you in Christ Jesus, you, too, can say with Luther and Habakkuk, and the poem writer:

"Thank You, God, for everything."

And mean it.

Gracious Father, we come asking Your forgiveness for the many times we complain about the circumstances of our lives. Turn our grumbling hearts into grateful hearts. Open our eyes to the evidence of Your love all around us. We know that every good and perfect gift comes from above. Remind us that every gift from above is good for us and is given to us because of Your per-

fect love for us in Jesus Christ Your Son, Our Lord. Thank You, God, for everything. In Jesus' name we pray. Amen.

Finding Hope

LEON. I'm but a stranger here, heaven is my home.

VAUGHN. What brought that on?

LEON. I've had a rough week. Some good friends of ours were killed last Monday on their way home from Arizona. Sometimes I have to remind myself that there is more to our existence than what happens here on earth.

JULIE. I need that reminder, too, Leon. I have a cousin struggling with cancer, and not a day goes by that I don't wonder why someone so young has to suffer like she does.

ESTELLE. It is different for those of us who are Christians, isn't it? I never realized how freeing it is to have a future in heaven. I don't worry about what will happen to me after I die, because I know I will be safe in the arms of Jesus.

LEON. The older I get, the more I look forward to the day I can be in heaven where there is no more sorrow or pain or sickness.

VAUGHN. It sounds kind of funny, but there are times that I look forward to dying too, Leon. I never thought I'd say that, but I mean it in a way that expresses my faith. I mean,

I don't want to die just yet, but I guess I'm not afraid to die either.

JULIE. St. Paul said that very thing in Philippians: "For to me, to live is Christ, to die is gain."

LEON. Sometimes we take our citizenship in heaven for granted. I know I find hope in a lot of tough situations that others find hopeless.

ESTELLE. My next door neighbor has never had time for religion. She actually told me that once. Now I heard she's having some serious health problems. This conversation makes me realize how frightened she must be. I think I'll give her a call this week.

VAUGHN. We're just strangers on this earth. Our real home is in heaven where there is no sorrow or sickness or death. But I know that God will always see me through the hard times here on earth.

LEON. My hope is in the Lord.

Finding Hope

The LORD is close to the brokenhearted and saves
those who are crushed in spirit.

Psalm 34:18

My friend, Mary Ann, told of a particularly bad asthma
attack that left her low. Feeling helpless made her feel hopeless, as well. Always a person with an inquiring mind, Mary
Ann got out her dictionary and looked up the word "hope."

Her research uncovered several important truths. First
of all, she found that "hope" contained two distinct elements:
expectation and desire. And secondly, she discovered that a
loss of either one of these ingredients (either expectation or
desire) could lead to a loss of "hope."

The Bible has many accounts of people who lost hope.
The story of God's promise to Abraham that he would be the
father of a great nation is a familiar one. Sarah, Abraham's
wife, laughed when the angel announced that their promised
son would arrive within the year. Though she desired a son,
she had long ago lost the expectation that God would fulfill
that particular promise. Desire without expectation equals
loss of hope.

After Moses led the Children of Israel out of slavery in
Egypt and the first flush of freedom was over, the people

began grumbling. "If only we had died by the Lord's hand in Egypt. There we sat around pots of meat and ate all the food we wanted." (Isn't this the same group that was starving and being worked to death only months earlier?) They go on, "But you have brought us out into this desert to starve this entire assembly to death" (Exodus 16:2–3). The people of Israel expected they would continue to be free; they had just lost all desire to do so. They no longer wished for the new life facing them. Expectation without desire equals loss of hope.

The journey to rediscover hope is beautifully told in the book of Ruth. It's the story of Naomi, who journeys with her husband and two sons to Moab because of a drought in Israel. Naomi's husband and sons die in Moab, the country in which they had hoped to find a better life. Totally bereaved, Naomi returns to Judah, bringing her daughter-in-law, Ruth, with her.

Her friends and neighbors, happy to see her, exclaim, "Can this be Naomi?" (Ruth 1:19).

But she responds without joy. "Don't call me, Naomi," she told them. (Naomi means "pleasant.") "Call me Mara because the Almighty has made my life very bitter" (Ruth 1:20). (Mara means "bitter.") Naomi did not expect life in her homeland would be any better than it had been in Moab.

But Naomi's daughter-in-law, Ruth, comes back from gleaning in the field of Boaz and tells Naomi a wonderful story of how kindly Boaz, a relative of Naomi's husband, has behaved toward her. Naomi catches a glimmer of hope. "[The

Lord] has not stopped showing His kindness to the living and the dead" (Ruth 2:20).

Ruth later marries Boaz, and they have a son, Obed. The women of the village exclaim, "Praise be to the Lord who this day has not left you without a kinsman-redeemer" and "Naomi has a son" (Ruth 4:14, 17).

Hope is rekindled. Naomi's life takes an unbelievable twist. This woman, whose only living relatives were two distant cousins, finds a new reason to live. "Naomi has a son."

For the Christian, knowing God has plans for the future can be enough, even when things seem hopeless from a human perspective. Ultimately, all hope comes from God. The psalmist proclaims, "The eyes of all look to you" (Psalm 145:15).

Jeremiah, God's prophet, under great persecution during the dark days of Israel, explains what sustains him:

> But this I call to mind and therefore have hope. Because of the Lord's great love we are not consumed, for His compassions never fail. They are new every morning; great is your faithfulness. I say to myself, "The Lord is my portion; therefore I will wait for Him."
>
> Lamentations 3:21–23

The psalmist agrees: "I wait for the Lord, my soul waits, and in His word I put my hope" (Psalm 130:1). Perhaps the key word here is "wait." Waiting for the Lord can mean waiting for hope to return. Because of God's great love for us in Christ, we know He has a plan for us, and we steadfastly believe in that plan, even through the dark times.

Expectation plus desire equals hope. And expectation, brought into line with God's plan, plus desire, according to His will, equals a lively hope that springs eternal in the trusting Christian's heart.

Gracious Father, we confess that we are often people of little faith. When the hard times come, we sometimes doubt Your love for us. We feel betrayed and abandoned. We lose hope. We come asking for Your forgiveness for these times of despair. Teach us to be patient, to trust Your promise to never leave us or forsake us. Ease the pain of our suffering. May Your strength be sufficient for all our needs, for our hope is in You alone. We ask in the name of Your Son, Jesus. Amen.

True Love

VAUGHN. I know we need to tell other people about our faith, but I don't think we should try to shove it down their throats.

LEON. Why do you say that?

VAUGHN. Well, my wife keeps trying to get me to invite our neighbors to come to church with us. They're great people. The thing is, we don't ever see them leave their house on a Sunday morning, but, that's their choice, isn't it?

ESTELLE. Have you ever asked them about their beliefs?

JULIE. But that's just it. Should we be questioning people about stuff like that? Doesn't that invade their privacy somehow?

LEON. I remember asking my dad about this a long time ago. He asked me if I thought it would be invading the privacy of a person with a severe case of pneumonia to tell them about penicillin.

ESTELLE. You mean, telling them about something that they might not have heard of that could save their life?

LEON. Right. Would you be trying to force your opinion on them?

VAUGHN. I get it. When I tell my neighbors what I know about Jesus, something that could make an eternal difference in their lives, they will either ask me for more information or reject the message. Either way, I have done the loving thing by offering them a way to escape eternal death.

JULIE. You've given me a whole new way of looking at this issue. I've often thought of joining the evangelism committee. When is the next meeting? I'd like to be a part of spreading that kind of love.

True Love

For everyone born of God overcomes the world. This is the victory that has overcome the world, even our faith. Who is it that overcomes the world? Only he who believes that Jesus is the Son of God. I write these things to you who believe in the name of the Son of God so that you may know that you have eternal life.

1 John 5:4–5, 13

Comforting words or harsh words? It depends on whether or not you believe that Jesus is the Son of God. This is the pivotal question for all mankind, for all peoples, for all places, for all time. Jesus reiterates this thought in John 3:16: he who believes is saved; he who does not believe perishes.

Some Christians would rather not believe in hell. It's a wonderful position to take; only it is not biblical. The Bible speaks of eternal punishment and, indeed, it is the reason we need a savior.

Only when we fully accept the truth about the realness of hell do we become eager to share our faith. Then we cannot wait to tell others the good news. We want them to know God has rescued us from eternal punishment.

Do we really think that our unsaved friends will suffer forever in eternity? If so, shouldn't we tell them about Jesus?

Shouldn't we invite them to church with us, or at least offer to drop their kids off at Sunday school? Shouldn't we be praying for them daily?

Billy Graham has said that one of the most powerful ways to spread the Gospel is still through Christian tracts. When we truly care about others, we might find ourselves mailing tracts with our bills or, perhaps, leaving tracts with a tip in the restaurants we frequent, in the hope that someone might come to believe the message of salvation. We might make an effort to send cards with a Christian message, and we might start speaking of our faith at work. Our deep concern for others will lead us to get the message out somehow because those who believe in Jesus are able to overcome the world and have eternal life. God has promised that once we speak up, He does the rest.

John frequently tells us to love one another in 1 John. "Dear friends, let us love one another, for love comes from God" (1 John 4:7). We show our love for others best when we share with them the Good News of the Gospel. Then others, too, can say:

We know also that the Son of God has come and has given us understanding, so that we may know him who is true. And we are in him who is true—even in his Son Jesus Christ. He is the true God and eternal life.

1 John 5:20

Heavenly Father, we say we are sinful and deserve nothing but punishment and death, yet in our sinfulness, we shy away from the reality of hell. We fail to tell others about Jesus because we don't really think that they are headed for eternal punishment. We have made You a God of tolerance, instead of a Holy God who is full of mercy. Open our eyes to see the true marvel of Your salvation. Give us a full understanding of the need for all to come to Christ to be rescued from the sentence of eternal death. Help us to love our unsaved friends enough to tell them the Good News of salvation through Christ, lest they perish in everlasting fire. We pray in the name of our only Redeemer, Jesus Christ. Amen.

Be Strong in the Lord

ESTELLE. I have a friend heading for trouble, and I just don't know what to do about it.

JULIE. What kind of trouble?

ESTELLE. Yesterday, she told me she was having a problem with the IRS about some back taxes she owes. She's been stressed out about this for over a year now, so she finally decided to pay the whole thing off at once and get it over with.

LEON. It's always a relief to have something like that taken care of.

ESTELLE. Sure, that pressure's off, but she owes back taxes because she is a poor manager of money and never has enough for these kinds of expenses. She's paying the minimum on her credit cards and has little credit left.

VAUGHN. I hope you didn't lend her the money, Estelle. If you did, I'm sure you'll never get it back. She'll have good intentions but, like she did with her other obligations, she'll just fall behind.

ESTELLE. No, she didn't get the money from me; *she took it from one of the accounts at work!* She said the temptation was just too great. She needed money desperately, and there sat the money, right at her fingertips. Of course, she plans to pay it back before anyone finds out.

JULIE. I'll bet Satan has been whispering that little solution in her ear for weeks. The sad thing is she doesn't really need money. What she needs is to learn how to *handle* money and how to trust that God will help her.

LEON. The devil tells us all kinds of lies. And they are usually something that makes our life seem easier or more pleasurable.

VAUGHN. And then the trap shuts, and the easy solution doesn't seem so easy anymore. Your friend could go to jail, you know, Estelle.

ESTELLE. No kidding. She's drifted away from her faith, so I know she's more vulnerable, and Satan knows it, too.

JULIE. We all need the whole armor of God if we are to be strong in the Lord.

Be Strong in the Lord

Finally, be strong in the LORD and in His mighty power. Put on the full armor of God so that you can take your stand against the devil's schemes. For our struggle is not against flesh and blood, but against the rulers, against the authorities, against the powers of this dark world and against the spiritual forces of evil in the heavenly realms. Therefore put on the full armor of God, so that when the day of evil comes, you may be able to stand your ground, and after you have done everything, to stand.

Ephesians 6:10–13

Preceding these verses in the sixth chapter of Ephesians, St. Paul gives directions for holy living to children, parents, slaves, and slave owners. Most of this instruction goes directly against our sinful nature. Children, honor your father and mother. Fathers, don't exasperate your children, but still, make sure they have proper training in the Lord. Slaves, obey your masters, just as you would obey Christ. Masters, treat your slaves as Christ would. Who can do all that? We are defeated before we begin.

And then we read the verses above and see their significance. Be strong *in the Lord*. Be strong in His mighty power.

This is why, as Christians, we are able to take our stand against the devil's schemes.

Paul seems to ask children, "Do you know how hard the devil works to make you angry with your parents? 'I hate you!' Have you ever said that to your mom or dad?"

He inquires of dads, "Do you know that there are principalities and powers scheming against you, telling you that your word is law; that when you speak, your children should blindly obey?"

He questions slaves, "Have you ever acknowledged that God has placed you in this position of humbleness? Satan is the one who shouts about individual rights and freedom for all. Do you really deserve any more than God has given?"

"Masters, don't you know that you are really God's slaves?" he asks. "Don't you realize that people are placed under you for you to serve them? Has the devil given you a different impression? Maybe suggesting that you are master; that you are above others, that people are your property?"

Paul wants to tell children that Mom and Dad are not out to get them. He reminds fathers that they are not doing battle against their children, but against the evil within both them and their children. He asks slaves and masters to consider, "Who is the real enemy here?"

St. Paul wants us to understand the personal battle against sin that we all face. It is more than the temptations around us that keep us from doing God's will. It is more than selfishness, and even more than our sinful nature. It is because we have a very real enemy who continually seeks our death and destruction. He is a dark and powerful enemy, one who hates good and loves evil.

So, says St. Paul, when the day of evil comes, you had better have a plan. If you want to stand in that day, you had better have on the whole armor of God. Be prepared to use the full arsenal of His weapons: the belt of truth, the breastplate of righteousness, the footwear of peace, the shield of faith, the helmet of salvation, and the sword of the Spirit. Pray. Stay alert. And pray some more. This is war. The enemy is fierce, and his hatred of God is all-consuming.

Gracious Father, You have promised us Your strength. You have offered us the full armor of God with which to do battle against forces that desire our death and destruction. Keep us from taking this warfare lightly. We thank and praise You for Your protection because we know that Satan's schemes assail us where and when we are most vulnerable.

Because of Your great love, through the sacrifice of our Lord Jesus Christ, we are able to "stand firm in the Lord" in times of temptation. May we be ever-mindful of the invitation to come to You in prayer and to cast our cares upon You. May Your strength be our strength and our salvation. We pray in Jesus' name. Amen.

They Hurried Off

LEON. Well, Julie, do you have big plans for Christmas?

JULIE. You bet I do. I've been working on the menu for Christmas dinner. All the presents are wrapped, and we are looking forward to the Christmas Eve service. I have enjoyed every minute of the preparations.

DANNY. Things are looking pretty good at our house too. We have our tree decorated, the presents are starting to pile up pretty well, and the smells from the kitchen are better every day. I love Christmas cookies.

VAUGHN. My brother and his wife and kids are coming to help us celebrate. How about you, Leon?

LEON. Things are looking and smelling pretty good at our house too.

JULIE. You're quiet this morning, Estelle. Is something wrong?

ESTELLE. Not at my house. I'm as excited as the rest of you. I was just thinking of my mother as you all talked about the planning and bustle at your homes.

DANNY. Is she sick or something?

ESTELLE. No, she's not sick, but she lives alone in another state. She doesn't get out much anymore. Most of her friends have died or are in nursing homes, and none of my brothers or sisters lives nearby.

JULIE. That's terrible. That means she has to spend Christmas all alone.

LEON. I suppose she finds Christmas a sad and lonely time.

DANNY. I never thought anyone would think of Christmas as a sad time.

ESTELLE. That's the reason I was thinking about her just now. I called yesterday and asked if she was lonely spending Christmas all by herself.

VAUGHN. I'm sure your call cheered her up a little.

ESTELLE. But that's just it. She wasn't the least bit sad or lonely. "Alone at Christmas?" she said. "Why would you think I was going to be alone when the whole point of Christmas is that God sent His Son to live with us and within us, so we would never be alone?" She said she was busy reading her Bible and listening to the Christmas carols on the radio to make sure all her preparations were done in time for Christmas.

VAUGHN. She still bakes cookies and stuff?

LEON. I think Estelle's mother meant that she was busy getting her heart ready to receive the Christ-child. Right, Estelle?

ESTELLE. Exactly right, Leon.

JULIE. Maybe we're not as ready for Christmas as I thought we were.

DANNY. Yeah, we better get busy and make sure our hearts are ready for Jesus.

They Hurried Off

So they hurried off and found Mary and Joseph, and the baby, who was lying in the manger.

Luke 2:16

I have always loved this verse of the Christmas story. Maybe it was one of my children's recitation verses for a Christmas program, or maybe it was even mine on some Christmas Eve long ago. It brings many images to mind of that wonderful night of the Savior's birth.

I picture the excited shepherds, the stable, the new parents, the manger, and, of course, the baby. My favorite part is imagining those rough working men rushing off to town in search of a baby. The clue from the angel was not a big one. "You will find a baby wrapped in cloths and lying in a manger" (Luke 2:12).

I know Bethlehem is called "O little town of Bethlehem" in the Christmas carol, but any town means buildings and people. On this night we know there were even more people in town than usual. That is why Mary and Joseph were in the stable in the first place. I wonder, did these shepherds have more information than we have from the Scripture story? Did they know which stable? Or did they rush headlong into the search, hoping for success, but not knowing whether they would find the baby or not?

We do know that they went. They heard the miraculous announcement of a Savior born for all people, and they went searching for Him. And faithful hearers continue to come seeking the Savior of the world.

Don't let the hustle and bustle of the season crowd out your dash to the Savior's manger. Drop what you are doing right this moment and go looking for Him. Prepare your heart to receive Him.

The shepherds went, perhaps knowing they would find Him, perhaps not. But we know we will find Him, for we have God's promise, "Ask and it will be given to you, seek and you will find" (Matthew 7:7). So this Christmas, spend time adoring the Christ Child, and become like the shepherds, who "returned, glorifying and praising God for all the things they had heard and seen, which were just as they had been told" (Luke 2:20).

Heavenly Father, today we are warmed by the physical evidence of Your love. Over the years men have longed to see the Messiah, already promised in the Garden of Eden. We rejoice, as did the shepherds, to see the Holy Child of Bethlehem. Fill our hearts and homes with the warmth of Your Love. May the coming of our Savior be the center of all our celebrations this Christmas, and make us heralds of Your salvation to all who will hear the message. We pray in the name of Jesus, the Babe of Bethlehem. Amen.

Standing Firm

LEON. Well, can you believe that another year is rolling around already? How was the last year for everyone?

ESTELLE. It was great for me. I had two new granddaughters.

DANNY. I got a puppy for Christmas this year. That makes it one of my best years so far.

ALAN. We've had a pretty rough year. In January, Lisa's mom had a stroke.

LISA. And the following March, Alan's brother was in a car accident. He got banged up pretty badly and was in the hospital for months afterward. To top it off, three days after Alan's brother's car accident, our dog, Shadow, was hit by a car and killed.

DANNY. Your dog got hit by a car?

ALAN. Then Lisa got laid off her job. That was a rough four months.

LISA. And last month Alan had back surgery.

LEON. This really has been a tough year for you two, hasn't it?

ESTELLE. I remember praying in church for your mom and Alan's brother, and even for your surgery, Alan. Didn't you ever ask where God was hiding this past year?

DANNY. Your dog died?

LEON. You must have felt like God was on vacation this year.

ALAN. I don't remember feeling that way at all. In fact, I think we felt God's presence in our lives more this year than any other.

ESTELLE. Yeah, but didn't you feel like God was turning a deaf ear to your prayers?

LISA. God doesn't promise to be our errand boy, Estelle. We don't just come to him with our prayers as demands and expect him to jump and fix things for us.

LEON. You're right, Lisa. God has promised to be there for us, but that doesn't mean keeping all sorrow and suffering away.

ALAN. Exactly, Leon. What He promises is just what we felt all year long. He promises to be with us in times of suffering, to give us His strength, and to make sure we know He loves us.

ESTELLE. This coming year may be a bad one for some of us, but with God's love, through Christ's atoning sacrifice, we are more than conquerors.

LISA. And nothing can separate us from the love of God in Christ Jesus.

DANNY. Your dog died?

Standing Firm

When the storm has swept by, the wicked are gone,
but the righteous stand firm forever.

Proverbs 10:25

When we read "when the storm has swept by" in this verse from Proverbs, many of us may think of the devastation that Hurricane Katrina brought to so many lives. Others immediately picture the personal losses they have experienced. Whether it is the loss of a job, the loss of health, or the loss of a loved one, the storms of life either knock us down, or we stand firm and are made stronger by them.

We know that in our own strength we can do nothing, but the mighty God of heaven has promised to never leave us or forsake us. The firm foundation on which we stand keeps us from being swept away. Many of us have experienced that strength, and we know it is something that exists apart from us. It is something that holds us firmly in place.

But the passage also says that after the storm, the wicked are gone. Gone? Perhaps the writer of Proverbs is implying that evil people do not stick around for the rebuilding part. That is probably true in the case of Hurricane Katrina. Countless numbers of Christian groups and good-hearted people have poured into that ravaged area to help, but, to my knowledge, there is no record of an organization that sends gang members into ravaged areas to clean out the muck.

Or perhaps the writer is implying that a storm can destroy the spirit of those who have been busy building lives of selfish gain. When all is taken away, they never quite recover. They simply give up and live in hopeless defeat.

Or maybe we are talking about end times—when we get to heaven the wicked will be no where to be found.

Whatever it means, the following words from St. Peter comfort our fearful hearts: "Once you were not a people, but now you are the people of God; once you had not received mercy, but now you have received mercy" (1 Peter 2:10).

When we received Jesus as our Savior from sin, He also became our Savior from the storms of life. What once would have swept us away into despair now makes us strong. And, except for the robe of righteousness from Jesus, we would be the ones who were "gone." "But thanks be to God! He gives us the victory through our Lord Jesus Christ" (1 Corinthians 15:57).

Jesus, Savior, pilot me
Over life's tempestuous sea;
Unknown waves before me roll,
Hiding rock and treacherous shoal.
Chart and compass come from Thee;
Jesus, Savior, pilot me.

As a mother stills her child,
Thou canst hush the ocean wild;
Boisterous waves obey Thy will,
When Thou sayest to them, "Be still!"
Wondrous Sovereign of the sea,
Jesus, Savior, pilot me.

Edward Hopper (1816–1888)

A Tiny Glimpse of Heaven

VAUGHN. Hey, Leon, don't you usually go south for a couple of weeks in the winter? It's Arizona, isn't it?

LEON. We decided not to go this year.

JULIE. I always envied your chance to escape winter, even for a little bit. Don't you often go to Texas, Estelle? That must make winter easier to take.

ESTELLE. We're not going south this year, either. It's funny, we loved being out of the cold, but we found that coming home to the rest of winter was awful.

LEON. We feel the same way. I know last year it was almost unbearable to revert to the cold after experiencing the easy, summer-type living.

JULIE. I never thought of it that way.

VAUGHN. Well, I guess I'm safe. I've never been to either Arizona or Texas during the winter, so how would I long for something I've never had?

LEON. Well, there is something I long for sometimes. And that's heaven.

VAUGHN. You want to die?

ESTELLE. I don't think that's what he meant, Vaughn, but I think I know what he is getting at.

JULIE. Me, too. I can be in the middle of the most awful day, and I'll find myself thinking how nice it is going to be in heaven. But I can be having a wonderful day, too, and, even in the middle a joyful time, a small voice in the back of my head says, "Is this the best it gets?" I still feel something is not quite perfect somehow.

LEON. That's exactly what I was trying to say, Julie. Even the good times are just a taste of things to come.

ESTELLE. I think that longing reminds us that we are just sojourners on this earth and, while we enjoy the journey, we long to be at our eternal home with our Heavenly Father.

JULIE. And here's another comforting thought, Estelle. Just like you hated coming back to winter, those who are already safely in heaven have no desire to come back to this life.

VAUGHN. I guess I *can* long for something I've never had. I'm looking forward to heaven too, Leon.

A Tiny Glimpse of Heaven

My prayer is not for them alone. I pray also for those who will believe in me through their message, that all of them may be one, Father, just as you are in me and I am in you. May they also be in us so that the world may believe that you have sent me. I have given them the glory that you gave me, that they may be one as we are one: I in them and you in me. May they be brought to complete unity to let the world know that you sent me and have loved them even as you have loved me. Father, I want those you have given me to be with me where I am, and to see my glory, the glory you have given me because you loved me before the creation of the world. Righteous Father, though the world does not know you, I know you, and they know that you have sent me. I have made you known to them, and will continue to make you known in order that the love you have for me may be in them and that I myself may be in them.

John 17:20–26

Jesus, ever obedient to His Father in heaven, has come to earth on a mission to save the world. He does this willingly, for He loves His Father, and He shares His Father's love for the world. He never falters in His purpose. Even in the Garden of Gethsemane, in an agony of prayer that the cup would be removed from Him, His resolve stays firm. "My Father, if it is not possible for this cup to be taken away unless I drink it, may your will be done" (Matthew 26:42).

This is the image of Jesus' sacrifice that comes most readily to mind: the obedient, suffering Savior. But in the verses from John's gospel above we see a different side of Jesus. Here is an animated Jesus, so in love with the Father, and so very excited about revealing that wonderful Father to the disciples, who, up to this point, have seen only a tiny glimmer of the Father's wonder and majesty.

These verses show us how eager Jesus was to tell the whole world of the wonderful glory He had seen. We see Him longing for men to realize the marvelous thing that has happened, that God so loved the world that He sent His only Son into the world for them.

He knows the world does not know the Father, but "I know You" (John 17:25), says Jesus, and He prays that the Father would reveal to men the joy of their salvation, that they might behold His glory.

And, when they finally get it, finally see God for who He is, finally see Him as Jesus sees Him, then they may be one with Jesus and the Father, just as Jesus and the Father are one. "That they may be one, as we are one." Oh, happy day!

Doesn't this prayer make you long for the day when we will know the Father as Jesus knows Him? Doesn't this take the sting out of dying? Doesn't it make you want to walk through that door of death right into the Father's loving arms? Is this a picture of heaven, or what?

Jesus prays, "Father, I want those you have given me to be with me where I am and to see my glory, the glory you have given me because you loved me before the creation of the world."

Me too. I want that too.

Thou art the Way, to thee alone
From sin and death we flee;
And all who would the Father seek,
Must seek him, Lord, by thee.

Thou art the Truth, thy word alone
True wisdom can impart;
Thou only canst inform the mind
And purify the heart.

Thou art the Life, the rending tomb
Proclaims thy conquering arm;
And those who put their trust in thee
Nor death nor hell shall harm.

Thou art the Way, the Truth, the Life:
Grant us that way to know,
That truth to keep, that life to win,
Whose joys eternal flow.

George Washington Duane (1799–1859)

The Perfect Prayer

JULIE. Boy, am I glad to be home.

LEON. I didn't know you were gone. Where have you been?

JULIE. I had to fly to Phoenix on a business trip.

ESTELLE. Wow. That would be great. I'd love a business trip to Phoenix in winter.

JULIE. You wouldn't have loved this trip.

VAUGHN. Oh, come on, Julie. Where's your sense of adventure? What could be that bad?

JULIE. I'm not sure if it was the fact that there was no one from the corporation to welcome me at the airport or the fact that when I finally managed to get to headquarters, the person with whom I was sent to negotiate refused to see me.

LEON. That's pretty rude. What did you do to tick the guy off?

JULIE. I didn't have to do anything. He was expecting my boss, so when I showed up, he took it as an insult. I guess his time was far too valuable for a "nobody" like me.

VAUGHN. That's harsh. How embarrassing. What did your boss say?

JULIE. He said to come straight home and he should have known better than to send someone as incompetent as I turned out to be. All in all, it was a humiliating experience.

ESTELLE. Boy, I'll bet you're glad to be home.

JULIE. Is there an echo in here?

LEON. Well, I'm glad Jesus is not like that. Can you imagine going to Him in prayer and finding out He doesn't think you're important enough to listen to?

VAUGHN. I've sometimes wondered if I should bother God with my problems. I mean, I'm me, and He is God. How do I know for sure He cares?

ESTELLE. Well, we know he cared about little children, and they were certainly not considered important in the adult world of Jesus' day.

JULIE. God's love for us in Jesus means that He never humiliates us just to feel better about Himself. I may refuse to go on any more business trips, but I never fear coming to my Heavenly Father in prayer.

The Perfect Prayer

In the same way, the Spirit helps us in our weakness. We do not know what we ought to pray for, but the Spirit himself intercedes for us with groans that words cannot express. And he who searches our hearts knows the mind of the Spirit, because the Spirit intercedes for the saints in accordance with God's will.

Romans 8:26–27

Have you ever been afraid to approach God with a petition? Maybe you were not sure that what you were going to ask for was His will for you? Perhaps you were being offered a job that would meet your career goals, but put a strain on your family. Or you were asked to accept a position within your church fellowship, and you did not want to do it.

What if you prayed about it and God saw through your motive? What if He knew that the answer you desired from Him was already decided in your mind? Would it be wrong to bring a concern to God, and then refuse to go where He led? Wouldn't it just be better to leave that situation out of your prayers, since you already knew what you were going to do anyway?

We ask ourselves these questions, and then along come the verses above in Romans 8. These are comforting words for the person praying. They encourage us to bring all our concerns to God because, you see, the Holy Spirit knows what is in our hearts. He knows our unholy motives and our sinful desires.

But He also knows that we desire to please and follow God. He knows what we need from God's hand to live a holy life. And so He changes our words and intercedes with the Father on our behalf.

But now our prayers have become holy prayers. "Because the Spirit intercedes for the saints in accordance with God's will."

Isn't that just the coolest thing? We can pray even though we do not know if we should, if we have ulterior motives or not, if we want to follow any path but our own. Because God hears our prayers in complete accordance with His will and, of course, the answer to the prayer will be yes. After all, He promises that if we ask anything according to His will, He will do it for us.

Knowing this drives us to our knees. There is no wrong way to pray. So bring it on. The Holy Spirit intercedes for us with proper prayers. And the answer to a proper prayer will always be in the affirmative. After all, there are only two answers to prayer: Yes or Something better.

The Holy Sprit intercedes for us in accordance with God's will, so there is no telling where our prayers will lead. And that is a good reason to bring everything to God in prayer.

Amen?

Amen.

Dear Heavenly Father, You are fully aware of our inner thoughts and desires. Many times we do not know how to pray. Our focus is so often on ourselves. Thank You for sending the Holy Spirit to change our selfish prayers to ones that unselfishly reflect Your will. Help us to be faithful in prayer, knowing that we are able to come to Your throne because of Christ's sacrifice on our behalf. We welcome the power of Your Holy Spirit to intercede for us so that our prayers become right prayers. In Jesus' name we pray. Amen.